D1604061

**Incarnate:
The Collected
Dead Man Poems**

Also by Marvin Bell

One of the Animals: Studio Improvisations, recorded 9 July 1992, with Mark Daterman, guitar, and Glen Moore, double bass, Musso Music (2019)

After the Fact: Scripts & Postscripts, with Christopher Merrill (2016)

Vertigo: The Living Dead Man Poems (2011)

Whiteout, with photographs by Nathan Lyons (2011)

A Primer about the Flag, with illustrations by Chris Raschka (for children) (2011)

7 Poets, 4 Days, 1 Book, with István László Geher, Ksenia Golubovich, Simone Inguanez, Christopher Merrill, Tomaž Šalamun, and Dean Young (2009)

Mars Being Red (2007)

Rampant (2004)

Nightworks: Poems 1962–2000 (2000)

Wednesday: Selected Poems 1966–1997 (1998, Europe)

Poetry for a Midsummer's Night, with paintings by Mary Powell (1998)

Ardor: The Book of the Dead Man, Volume 2 (1997)

A Marvin Bell Reader: Selected Poetry and Prose (1994)

The Book of the Dead Man (1994)

Iris of Creation (1990)

New and Selected Poems (1987)

Drawn by Stones, by Earth, by Things That Have Been in the Fire (1984)

Old Snow Just Melting: Essays and Interviews (1983)

Segues: A Correspondence in Poetry, with William Stafford (1983)

These Green-Going-to-Yellow (1981)

Stars Which See, Stars Which Do Not See (1977)

Residue of Song (1974)

The Escape into You (1971)

A Probable Volume of Dreams (1969)

Things We Dreamt We Died For (1966)

Incarnate:
The Collected
Dead Man Poems

Marvin Bell

COPPER CANYON PRESS
PORT TOWNSEND, WASHINGTON

Copper Canyon Press is in residence at Fort Worden State Park in Port Townsend, Washington, under the auspices of Centrum. Centrum is a gathering place for artists and creative thinkers from around the world, students of all ages and backgrounds, and audiences seeking extraordinary cultural enrichment.

LIBRARY OF CONGRESS CATALOGING-IN-PUBLICATION DATA
Names: Bell, Marvin, 1937– author.
Title: Incarnate: The collected dead man poems / Marvin Bell.
Description: Port Townsend, Washington : Copper Canyon Press, [2019]
Identifiers: LCCN 2019013620 | ISBN 9781556595837 (pbk. : alk. paper)
ISBN 9781556595820 (hardback : alk. paper)
Classification: LCC PS3552.E52 A6 2019 | DDC 811/.54—dc23
LC record available at https://lccn.loc.gov/2019013620

9 8 7 6 5 4 3 2 FIRST PRINTING

COPPER CANYON PRESS
Post Office Box 271
Port Townsend, Washington 98368
www.coppercanyonpress.org

Acknowledgments

Grateful acknowledgment is made to the editors of books and periodicals in which these poems, some in earlier versions, appeared previously:

AGNI, The American Poetry Review, Arch Literary Journal, Ardor: The Book of the Dead Man, Volume 2 (Copper Canyon), *Arroyo Literary Review, Audemus, The Bloomsbury Review, The Book of the Dead Man* (Copper Canyon), *BorderSenses, Boulevard, Breathe: 101 Contemporary Odes* (C&R Press), *Camoupedia: A Compendium of Research on Art, Architecture and Camouflage* (Bobolink Books), *Chance of a Ghost: An Anthology of Contemporary Ghost Poems* (Helicon Nine Editions), *The Coachella Review, Colorado Review, Contemporary American Poetry,* sixth edition (Houghton-Mifflin), *Cordite* (Australia), *Crazyhorse, Cutthroat, december, Denver Quarterly, Dog Music: A Poetry Anthology* (St. Martin's Press), *Ecotone, Electric Rexroth* (Japan), *Electronic Poetry Review, The Fiddlehead* (Canada), *Fifth Wednesday, Five Points, The Georgia Review, The Gettysburg Review, The Gift of Tongues: Twenty-Five Years of Poetry from Copper Canyon Press, Good Company: American Poets Born Between 1935 and 1945* (Maypop Press), Gray Spider Press (broadside), *The Great Blue Heron and Other Poems* (Adrienne Lee Press), *Great River Review, Green Mountains Review, Harvard Review, Hayden's Ferry Review, Hunger Mountain, Inertia, The Iowa Review, Iris of Creation* (Copper Canyon), *Left Bank, MAKE, Mars Being Red* (Copper Canyon), *A Marvin Bell Reader* (Middlebury College Press/University Press of New England), *The Massachusetts Review, Minutes of the Lead Pencil Club* (Pushcart Press), *Money* (Peregrine Smith), *Natural Bridge, New American Zeen, New England Review, New Poets of the American West* (Many Voices Press), *The New Republic, The New Yorker, Nine Mile, North American Review, The North Stone Review, One, ONTHEBUS, Orbis* (England), *Orion, Outsiders* (Milkweed Editions), *Phainomai* (Marrowstone Press), *Pleiades, A Poem of One's Own* (University Press of New England), *Poetry, Poetry East, Poetry Miscellany, Poetry Northwest, Prairie Schooner, Projector, Quarry West, Rattle, Rhetoric Review, RHINO Poetry, Sifrut, The Southern Review, spelunker flophouse, Telling and Remembering: A Century of American Jewish Poetry* (Beacon Press), *Trafika* (Prague), *Truth To Power* (Cutthroat), *Undocumented:*

Great Lakes Poets Laureate on Social Justice (Michigan State University Press), *Verse, Vertigo: The Living Dead Man Poems* (Copper Canyon), *Visiting Bob: Poems Inspired by the Life and Work of Bob Dylan* (New Rivers Press), *Visiting Dr. Williams: Poems Inspired by the Life and Work of William Carlos Williams* (University of Iowa Press), *Voices* (Australia), *Voices on the Landscape* (Loess Hills Press), *We Wanted To Be Writers* (Skyhorse Publishing), *Wednesday: Selected Poems 1966–1997* (Salmon Poetry, Ireland), *Western Humanities Review, What Will Suffice: Contemporary American Poets on the Art of Poetry* (Peregrine Smith), *Whiteout: Dead Man Poems by Marvin Bell in Response to Photographs by Nathan Lyons* (Lodima Press), *Willow Springs, The Writing Path* (University of Iowa Press), and *Xanadu 2* (Tor Books).

"The Book of the Dead Man (Collaboration)" was mounted for the Born installation and performance *The Eight Essential Ingredients,* Richard Hugo House, Seattle, 2006.

"Sounds of the Resurrected Dead Man's Footsteps (Abandonment of Distinctions)," part 10 of "Journal of the Posthumous Present," commissioned by the Getty Research Institute to reflect the Institute's theme for 2001–2002, "Frames of Viewing: Perception, Experience, Judgment," composed entirely of lines from Dead Man poems, appears in *Rampant* (Copper Canyon, 2004).

Dorothy
Nathan, Leslie, Colman, Aileen
Jason, Sheila

The point of philosophy is to start with something so simple as not to seem worth stating, and to end with something so paradoxical that no one will believe it.

Bertrand Russell

Contents

2. Ardor: The Book of the Dead Man, Volume 2 (1997)

3. *from* Mars Being Red (2007)

4. Vertigo: The Living Dead Man Poems (2011)

5. New and Uncollected

Author's Preface

I would like readers of this volume to think of it as a lifetime book, not of the lifetime of the writer but of the reader, hence a book to be read over time, to dip in and out of. For me, it has been a form for truth and defiance, begun in joy and verbal music, in the face of the inevitability of death and the kaleidoscopic nature of perception. It is life amid the dark matter and sticky stuff. It voices a way to live there.

I have been asked if I am the Dead Man. No, but he knows a lot about me. Are the poems chock-full of autobiography? Yes, but it is not presented as such and asks no credit. The Dead Man is not a persona but an overarching consciousness. He is alive and dead at once, defeating time.

I waited four years after writing the first Dead Man poem, or perhaps being found by it, before writing another. A couple more, and the form had hooked me with its music and capacity. I wrote the first of these poems at age fifty-three and the last at age eighty-one. Blessings on the reader who leans forward.

A note about what is included here. *Incarnate: The Collected Dead Man Poems* incorporates only the first four of the twenty-four poems from the 2011 book *Whiteout,* a volume of Dead Man poems written in response to photographs by Nathan Lyons. I felt that those four ("Light Skeleton," "Big Eyes," "Whiteout," and "The Palm") could stand alone, as they did in 2011 in *Vertigo,* while the other twenty are best read in direct relation to the photos to which they responded.

M. B.

Incarnate: The Life of the Dead Man

David St. John

For more than twenty-five years the Dead Man has lived among us. For those readers who, from the very first, recognized that the Dead Man was also living *within* us, it has been astonishing to watch as Marvin Bell created poem by poem, book by book, one of the most powerful bodies of poetry (this collection, *Incarnate,* is the Dead Man's body) in late twentieth-century and early twenty-first-century American literature. No voice in our poetry has spoken with more eloquence and wisdom about the daily spiritual, political, and psychological erosion in our lives; no poet has gathered our American experience with a more capacious tenderness—all the while naming and celebrating our persistent hopes and enduring human desires.

When the Dead Man embraces us in these pages, he also breathes into us faith in ourselves, a resurrected belief in our own ability to reckon—as he himself does with his wry humor and brilliant yet simple grace, illuminating the complexity of our lives as they have seemed to fragment around us. If we somehow feel we have lost our way along whatever paths we have traveled, the Dead Man arises as the lens through which we can see those tumbling pieces in the kaleidoscope—those jagged shards of personal experience or of historical or social wreckage—resolve into focus.

Throughout his career, Marvin Bell has always brought to his poetry a devotion to the lyric intensity of Dickinson as well as the broadly woven gestural expansiveness of Whitman. He has always echoed the performative genius of John Berryman alongside the postapocalyptic vaudeville of Samuel Beckett. In the Dead Man poems, as he rehearses the Zen admonition *Live as if you were already dead*, Bell employs a wicked humor as deeply American as Mark Twain's (or Lenny Bruce's) yet as intimate and local as Buster Keaton's. He has always shared Wallace Stevens's elegant philosophical impulses and his attention to the beauty of thought and of the mind in process. The steady political current in Bell's poetry is as charged as Muriel Rukeyser's, and his unapologetic antiwar evisceration of American policies is as radical as that of any poet who came of age after World War II. His Bush-era poems are, in my view, the very best we have from that period of our history. It's also time Bell's deep love of William Carlos Williams (and the American vernacular) as well as his admiration for the Beat poets, especially Allen Ginsberg, be recognized as crucial elements in his poetry. From the beginning of his writing life, Bell understood the consolation of mystery in poetry and the lasting power and presence of art. Still, let's be clear: Bell's Dead Man only appears detached by virtue of our own definition of death; the Dead Man of these poems is ever of this dark world and its sorrows. To be alive, the Dead Man knows, is to die a little every day, even if—so unlike us—the Dead Man can no longer be betrayed by anything living.

Bell's poetry has always exhibited a profoundly metaphysical intelligence. In the poems of the Dead Man, Bell has created a conversational and reflective philosophical music, establishing (as a formal choice) the poetic sentence as a measure of his poetic line. There is a declarative ease to this work that enables the poems to double back on themselves. The Dead Man poems are insistently bifocal and riddled with the dualities of experience. Perhaps it was Bell's history as a photographer that in part motivated the distinctive "twin-lens reflex" modality of his Dead Man poems, yielding a fierce clarity from dual perspectives. For the Dead Man, paradox and duality constitute philosophical and moral clarity. Indeed, in one of *Incarnate*'s signature poems, Bell says of the Dead Man, "Like a camera, he squints to lengthen the depth of his field and bring the future into focus."

The poems of the Dead Man are the living end. They are multivalent and protean, yet immediate and conversational. Even with the scent of the earth and its humus clinging to him (post-humus, as in: resurrected), the Dead Man is the oracle of the everyday. The Dead Man lives within the Taoist vision of the world of the ten thousand things. The Dead Man lives without us, of course, yet also within us.

Remarkable for its eclectic and culturally diverse vision, *Incarnate* embodies a vivid world of poetic reflection unlike anything else in American poetry.

Incarnate:
The Collected
Dead Man Poems

The Book of the Dead Man

(1994)

Live as if you were already dead.
(Zen admonition)

Preface

Before the Dead Man, minus-1 was still an imaginary number.

The Dead Man will have nothing more to do with the conventional Ars Poetica, that blind manifesto allegiant to the past. Let the disenchanted loyalist reconsider the process. Among motives, occasions, codes, needs and knucklehead accidents, the Dead Man accepts all and everything. He knows in his bones that writing is metabolic.

What are we to make of the Dead Man's reference to Keats? That poetry should come, as Keats wrote, "as naturally as the Leaves to a tree"? To this the Dead Man has added the dimension of the minus. He understands that fallibility and ignorance are the true stores, the bottomless reservoirs of creation. He is the fount *for* that spillover. As for the tedium of objects distorted from their long imprisonment in books, the Dead Man has learned that to be satiated is not to be satisfied.

So he furthers the love affair between the sentence and the line. Whereas formerly the line took a missionary position, under the rule of the Dead Man the sentence once more invigorates the line. The ongoing attempt by dictionary makers to define "poetry," as it has been called, is an object of derision to the Dead Man. The Dead Man knows that every technique is passé except when reencountered at its birth. The Dead Man moves as comfortably among nightingales as among house wrens.

"Perfected fallibility": that's the key, the solace, the right number (one of one, two of two, three of three, etc.). Hence, the fragment is more than the whole. The Dead Man is a material mystic. His hourglass is bottomless. No. 27 ("About the Dead Man and *The Book of the Dead Man*") reminds us that the Dead Man is "a postscript to closure," and "the resident tautologist in an oval universe that is robin's-egg-blue to future generations."

Has it not already been stated of the Dead Man in the poem "About the Dead Man and His Poetry" that he is the tautologist, the postscript, perfected fallibility, etc.? Yes. The Dead Man tells the truth the first time. The Dead Man, too, writes as he has to—with a watch cap and a sweatshirt, with a leaking skull and dilapidated lungs, at an hour beyond clocks. He lives on hunger. He eats his words.

Before the birth of the Dead Man, it was not possible to return. It was not possible, it was preconceptual, it was discretionary to the point of chaos and accident to return, since of course there was nowhere yet to return to. Since the birth of the Dead Man, however, it is possible, even likely, that one may return. From the future, one walks ever more slowly into the past.

All this the Dead Man knows. As for me, I know nothing. But do not think one can know nothing so easily. It has taken me many years.

M. B.

The Book of the Dead Man

The Book of the Dead Man (#1)

1. About the Dead Man

The dead man thinks he is alive when he sees blood in his stool.

Seeing blood in his stool, the dead man thinks he is alive.

He thinks himself alive because he has no future.

Isn't that the way it always was, the way of life?

Now, as in life, he can call to people who will not answer.

Life looks like a white desert, a blaze of today in which nothing distinct can
    be made out, seen.

To the dead man, guilt and fear are indistinguishable.

The dead man cannot make out the spider at the center of its web.

He cannot see the eyelets in his shoes and so wears them unlaced.

He reads the large type and skips the fine print.

His vision surrounds a single tree, lost as he is in a forest.

From his porcelain living quarters, he looks out at a fiery plain.

His face is pressed against a frameless window.

Unable to look inside, unwilling to look outside, the man who is dead is like
    a useless gift in its box waiting.

It will have its yearly anniversary, but it would be wrong to call it a holiday.

2. More About the Dead Man

The dead man can balance a glass of water on his head without trembling.
He awaits the autopsy on the body discovered on the beach beneath
      the cliff.
Whatever passes through the dead man's mouth is expressed.
Everything that enters his mouth comes out of it.
He is willing to be diagnosed, as long as it won't disturb his future.
Stretched out, he snaps back like elastic.
Rolled over, he is still right-side-up.
When there is no good or bad, no useful or useless, no up, no down, no
      right way, no perfection, then okay it's not necessary that there be
      direction: up is down.
The dead man has the rest of his life to wait for color.
He finally has a bird's-eye view of the white-hot sun.
He finally has a complete sentence, from his head to his feet.
He is, say, America, but he will soon be, say, Europe.
It will be necessary merely to cross the ocean and pop up in the new land,
      and the dead man doesn't need to swim.
It's the next best thing to talking to people in person.

The Book of the Dead Man (#2)

1. First Postscript: About the Dead Man

The dead man thinks he is alive when he hears his bones rattle.

Hearing his bones rattle, the dead man thinks he is alive.

He thinks himself alive because, what else would he think?

Now he can love and suffer, as in life, and live alone.

The dead man no longer hears the higher register of the chandelier.

The dead man listens for pedal notes and thunder, tubas and bassoons.

He reads lips without telling anyone, but others know.

He can no longer scratch his back so he stands near walls.

To the dead man, substance and meaning are one.

To the dead man, green and black are not estranged, nor blue and gray, nor
    here and there, nor now and then.

The dead man has separate sets of eyes for here and there.

In the dead man's world, all time and stories are abstract.

In a concrete house with real walls, he lies down with the news.

The screen's flickering pixels are to him eyelets through which the world
    each morning is laced up for the day.

The dead man rises from his bed at night with great effort.

He is a rolling map of veins, a hilly country built on flatland.

The map of the body is of no use to the dead man.

When the dead man turns his neck, it's something to see from a distance.

2. Second Postscript: More About the Dead Man

Asleep, the dead man sinks to the bottom like teeth in water.
Whatever came to be by love or entropy, all that sprouted and grew, all that
      rotted and dissolved, whatever he saw, heard, felt, tasted or smelled,
      every wave and breeze has its metabolic equivalent in his dreams.
He is the bones, teeth and pottery shards to be claimed eons hence.
He is the multifaceted flag of each deciduous tree, reenacting time.
The dead man will not go away, the dead man holds up everything with his
      elegant abstentions.
All his life he had something to say and a string on his finger.
The dead man will be moving to Florida or Maine, or sailing to California,
      or perhaps he is staying put.
He has only to say where he wishes to be, and it can be arranged.

Inside the dead man, there is still a mellow sparking of synapses.
Unsent messages pool on the wavery deck, hit tunes that would last forever,
      jokes that never staled.
The dead man is an amphitheater of dramatic performances, ethereal scripts
      now written in the air like used radio signals in space.
The dead man mistakes natural disasters for applause—erosion in Carolina,
      quakes in California.
The dead man's shoes are muddy from being constantly on stage.

The Book of the Dead Man (#3)

1. About the Beginnings of the Dead Man

When the dead man throws up, he thinks he sees his inner life.
Seeing his vomit, he thinks he sees his inner life.
Now he can pick himself apart, weigh the ingredients, research
    his makeup.
He wants to study things outside himself if he can find them.
Moving, the dead man makes the sound of bone on bone.
He bends a knee that doesn't wish to bend, he raises an arm that
    argues with a shoulder, he turns his head by throwing it wildly
    to the side.
He envies the lobster the protective sleeves of its limbs.
He believes the jellyfish has it easy, floating, letting everything pass
    through it.
He would like to be a starfish, admired for its shape long after.
Everything the dead man said, he now takes back.
Not as a lively young man demonstrates sincerity or regret.
A young dead man and an old dead man are two different things.
A young dead man is oil, an old dead man is water.
A young dead man is bread and butter, an old dead man is bread and
    water—it's a difference in construction, also architecture.
The dead man was there in the beginning: to the dead man, the sky is
    a crucible.
In the dead man's lifetime, the planet has changed from lava to ash
    to cement.
But the dead man flops his feathers, he brings his wings up over his head
    and has them touch, he bends over with his beak to the floor, he folds
    and unfolds at the line where his armor creases.
The dead man is open to change and has deep pockets.
The dead man is the only one who will live forever.

2. More About the Beginnings of the Dead Man

One day the dead man looked up into the crucible and saw the sun.
The dead man in those days held the sky like a small globe, like a patchwork
    ball, like an ultramarine bowl.
The dead man softened it, kneaded it, turned it and gave it volume.
He thrust a hand deep into it and shaped it from the inside out.
He blew into it and pulled it and stretched it until it became full-sized, a
    work of art created by a dead man.
The excellence of it, the quality, its character, its fundamental nature, its
    raison d'être, its "it" were all indebted to the dead man.

The dead man is the flywheel of the spinning planet.
The dead man thinks he can keep things the same by not moving.
By not moving, the dead man maintains the status quo at the center of
    change.
The dead man, by not moving, is an explorer: he follows his nose.
When it's not personal, not profound, he can make a new world anytime.
The dead man is the future, was always the future, can never be the past.
Like God, the dead man existed before the beginning, a time marked by
    galactic static.
Now nothing remains of the first static that isn't music, fashioned into
    melody by the accidents of interval.
Now nothing more remains of silence that isn't sound.
The dead man has both feet in the past and his head in the clouds.

The Book of the Dead Man (#4)

1. Shoes, Lamp and Wristwatch

The dead man has a fixation on shoes.
Seeing his shoes, he cannot take his eyes off them.
Shoes, lamp and wristwatch—these are the basics, the elements, the factors.
The dead man factors-in time, light and travel.
So much depends on going, seeing and knowing: shoes, lamp
    and wristwatch.
The dead man embodies light and time at a distance: shoes, lamp and
    wristwatch.
The dead man wears his heart on his sleeve, but it's not what you think.
On the dead man's stopped watch, the time is always right.
The dead man's lamp is a dead man's lamp—on or off.
The dead man's ill-fitting footwear is never uncomfortable.
Long since the dead man made a fetish of entropy—shoes, lamp and
    wristwatch.

2. More About the Dead Man's Shoes, Lamp and Wristwatch

The dead man's shoes are two columns of x's, two fabricated facts, two tricks
     propped up by the heels.
The dead man's lamp is a hole in the roof, a gossamer shaft, a porous umbrella.
The dead man's wristwatch is a plaque with straps, a black-and-white picture
     of local knowledge.
The dead man learns by looking up and down, he values stamina, he assumes
     that all stories are apocryphal.
Thus, the dead man's time is time and no time, his lamp is light and no light,
     and his two shoes do not prevent his two feet from touching the earth.
By fictive lamplight, on the days of the mythic calendar, the dead man stands
     upright but weightless in his still-beautiful shoes.

The Book of the Dead Man (#5)

1. About the Dead Man and Pain

When the dead man's ankle breaks, he is stoical.
Being stoical, the dead man is not hobbled by a broken ankle.
The dead man doesn't fear pain; he simply has no use for it.
When he breaks an ankle, he uses the other one.
When he breaks both ankles, he uses his arms, etc.
The dead man is like quadriplegics who grip the paintbrush with their teeth,
    the paralyzed who sip and puff to get around in their chairs.
Language lingers in the dead man after the event.
In his pre-Socratic period, the dead man raced against Achilles.
You thought I was going to say he raced against time, but no, it was Achilles,
    Achilles-the-Warrior, Achilles-the-Fleet, Achilles-the-Unbeatable.
Zeno-the-Philosopher gave the signal to start, and the dead man inched
    forward.
Achilles thought about running but did not move, he considered starting
    but did not take a step, he wondered about his indecision but did not
    contract a muscle.
Thus it was that the dead man, slow of foot, defeated Achilles.
Hence it came to pass that Achilles fell to a dead man, one of the precursor
    events of the future in which the dead man would forever be victorious.

2. More About the Dead Man and Pain

The dead man's condition is chronic, no longer acute, a constant state
of being.
Because the dead man is in a constant state of being, his condition is
chronic, no longer acute.
He thinks that language will be the death of us so he prefers gestures.
Now he points by implication, directs by nuance, gathers and distributes
atoms of information, the vapor of data, the ether of ions—all without
changing his position.
Pain to the dead man mirrors his long refusal, his wordless challenge to the
burning ceiling he used to call "sky."
The dead man spits in the eye of pain, he dismisses it with a gesture.
When the dead man thinks about pain, he thinks about being alive, that's
how he knew he was.
When there is no pain, no welcoming, no hospitality, no disdain, there's
no need to be stoical, the opportunity itself becomes disingenuous,
emotion embodied in all things including gases.
When there is no pain, no fallacy is pathetic.
The dead man argues to lose, he articulates his ideas only to see them
blurred, he expresses himself knowing his works are being written
to be erased.
The dead man behaves stoically only because he thinks it to be the final
proof of life.
In his unfeeling comprehension of pain, the dead man behaves as if it hurts.
The dead man is like a stone reduced to tears.

The Book of the Dead Man (#6)

1. About the Dead Man's Speech

Will the dead man speak? Speak, says the lion, and the dead man makes the
    sound of a paw in the dirt.
When the dead man paws the dirt, lions feel the trembling of the pride.
Speak, says the tree, and the dead man makes the sound of tree bark
    enlarging its circumference, a slight inhalation.
Speak, says the wind, and the dead man exhales all at once.
Whoever told the dead man to be quiet was whistling in the dark.
To the dead man, the dark is all words as white is all colors.
The dead man obliges, he cooperates, he speaks when spoken to, so when
    the dirt says Speak, he says what erosion says.
And when the air says Speak, the dead man says what a cavity says.
The dead man knows the syntax of rivers and rocks, the one a long ever-
    qualifying sentence for which no last words suffice, the other the
    briefest and most steadfast exercise in exclusion.
The dead man is a rock carried by a river, a pebble borne by air, a sound
    carved into frequencies infrequently registered.

2. More About the Dead Man's Speech

The dead man is part of the chorus that sings the music of the spheres.

Dead man's music uses the harmonics and parasitics of sound, in bands of
low frequencies caught in ground waves that hug the terrain as they go,
and in ultrahigh megacycles that dent the ionosphere and refract over
the horizon.

The dead man makes no distinction between the music he hears and the
music he only knows about.

There are five elements in the dead man's music (time, tempo, key, harmony
and counterpoint) and two factors (silence and chance).

To the dead man, the wrinkled back of a hand is a score to be read.

The balding top and back of his head are a kind of braille awaiting a blind
conductor.

The dead man's bone-sounds and teeth-clacks are a form of tuning up.

Sad music brings artificial tears to the dead man's dilated eyes.

All things being equal, the dead man is not fussy about pitch and dissonance.

His inner ear is set to hear euphonic consonants.

The dead man sings in the shower, in good weather and bad, without
knowing a song.

He hums the tunes of commercials without the words, sympathetic
vibrations.

He has ideas for musical instruments made of roots and feathers, harps that
use loose dirt something like an interrupted hourglass.

When the dead man, in a gravelly voice, sings gospel, hammers descend
upon anvils.

The Book of the Dead Man (#7)

1. About the Dead Man and the National Pastime

When the dead man sees a rock, he remembers the hidden ball trick.
Remembering the hidden ball trick, the dead man sees a rock.
Now he can pick it up and throw it to no one, the *acte gratuit.*
Now he can make them pay dearly for the long lead off first.
The hidden ball trick is subterfuge, but so what?, nothing the dead man
     does violates the spirit of the game.
The dead man practices the decoy, forcing runners to slide.
Running from third for home with one out, tie score, bottom of the ninth,
     he delays, then bowls over the catcher, letting the runner from second
     score between his legs.
He steals second, then steals first, second, first, until the catcher throws
     wildly into the outfield and a runner scores from third.
He throws a potato back to the pitcher after a pickoff play.
He drops his bat in the batting box and takes a miniature step backward to
     cause a balk.
The dead man feels the spirit of the game in his bones.
He understands the long windup, the walk to the mound, the interval
     between hit and error, the stopped seams on a hanging curve.
The dead man knows why the players don't step on the chalk lines as they
     change from out to up and up to out.

2. More About the Dead Man and the National Pastime

The dead man remembers the great individualists: Ruth swinging just
    beneath his potbelly, DiMaggio's spread stance, Williams' super-vision,
    Reiser hitting the outfield walls to catch flies before padding, Newsom
    sitting down after whiffing and then trying to run for it from the
    dugout, Musial coiled at bat like a question mark, Satchel Paige above
    all who said not to look back, Lopat's junk, Veeck's midget, the spit and
    Vaseline specialists, the cutters.
The dead man can go on and on if it goes into extra innings.
To the dead man, a good arm means more than a good stick.
The dead man likes scoreless games with plenty of runners.
The dead man stands in the on-deck circle admiring the trademark of
    his bat.
He sights along the handle, he taps it to listen for cracks, he rubs pine tar up
    and down oozing with anticipation.
The inning ends before the dead man can bat.
If it takes a great play, a double play, a triple play, no matter what, the dead
    man beats the curfew.
The dead man died from pennant fever but was resurrected by a Texas
    League pop-up which landed nearby and which he is keeping hidden
    until the end of the seventh-inning stretch.

The Book of the Dead Man (#8)

1. About the Dead Man's Head

The dead man puts another head on his shoulder and thinks he's a Siamese
twin.

He thinks he's a Siamese twin when he puts another head on his shoulder.

"Double or nothing" is the dead man's motto.

He has other mottoes: "A stitch in time sews heaven to earth" and "No pain,
no end to pain."

The dead man thinks he's a Siamese twin because one head cannot hold
everything he is feeling.

The dead man has migraines from too much data, pinpricks of discrete
events in the metaphysical.

Random neural firings in the dead man produce predictive dreams among
an infinite number of occasions, occurrences, chances, so why not
double it.

Musketry and bee sounds in the dead man's ears are penny ante compared
to the wealth of petrified knowledge he already contains.

2. More About the Dead Man's Head

When the dead man stays up too late, his brain empties out, *whoosh.*

When the dead man's brain makes that sound, *whoosh,* it empties out.

The dead man knows it's late but not how late, he likes the people who come
    to see him but doesn't know who they are, he is old and senses that he
    needs a fresh brain.

The dead man holds up a skull and addresses himself, like Hamlet, but the
    words "to be or not to be" ring hollow.

No tragedy can occur unless the dead man can fall from a high place.

It will take years to stage the event: a calving glacier, a bursting volcano, a
    sudden fissure into which fall the flaws of temporal foundations.

A former tragedian, the dead man undergoes a change of heart.

The dead man's laughter increases in the abscesses and hollows, his body is a
    corridor of comedy, his cavernous hilarity wreaks havoc among
    the divisive.

When the comic and tragic split, the dead man feels like Siamese twins.

The presence of the dead man means two of everything.

The Book of the Dead Man (#9)

1. About the Dead Man and Nature

When the dead man emerges in high grass, he thinks he sees his shadow.
Thinking he sees his shadow, the dead man emerges in waist-high grass.
The dead man has sewn dunes in Indiana, set pine groves in New Jersey,
     combed tidal flats in Washington, chipped the rocky flanks of Oregon
     and Maine, twisted seaweed in the Pacific, constellated Atlantic
     beaches in fossil teeth: the dead man knows the land firsthand.
The dead man has been swept by date palms, fig trees, weeping willows, live
     oak, he has felt beach grass and kudzu, he has crossed lava and baked
     sand: the dead man's understanding blankets the planet.
The dead man has seen the green wink of the declining sun.
To the dead man, fog is a mirror, a buttress against the distance.
The dead man's face appears to him among the clouds.
The dead man knows what he looks like in all things because, who would
     better?
To the question, Why is the dead man the conscience of the planet, the dead
     man's refusal to reply constitutes a final why not?
The dead man's didactics have an air of criminal vinegar.
The dead man, thought to be disintegrating, dissolving and deconstructing,
     all the while has been materializing, coalescing and under-structuring.
His is the composition of heavenly music, atomic constellations echoing that
     subatomic groundwork for which he is better known.
Without the dead man, the sunflower would not proclaim its common face,
     nor the lily sway into biblical cover.
Freeze the dead man out and the natural world stops making love and
     babies.
But include the dead man, invite his willing reticence that bespeaks
     essence to the core, and the world oozes with spring and love songs
     to Proserpine.
Eurydice depends on the dead man too.

2. More About the Dead Man and Nature

Under his Malthusian covers, all is not lost.

Where survival of the fittest still reigns, the weak shall inherit.

Neither your friends nor the dead man's but someone's shall creep from the
    dank underside of wishes into the telling gift of then.

Nor shall the dead man be any the less for it.

For then shall the dead man come true, in every form of the invisible.

The hole shall be greater than any particle.

The present shall be greater than the future and the past greater than
    the present.

Such is the dead man's hindsight that can cap the lily with its own birth,
    unhook the atoms of a boulder, and turn the sea to seabed.

The dead man has experienced the future, what others see merely as the
    dark at the bottom of the stairs.

All is natural to the dead man.

"For that is what men do," says the dead man.

All men and women are in his thoughts today.

All are swept by the weeping willow where they lie hugging the dirt to
    stay low.

All but the dead man shall bow down before plenty.

All but the dead man shall bow down for nothing.

The Book of the Dead Man (#10)

1. About the Dead Man and His Poetry

The dead man has poetry in his stomach, bowels and genitals.
In the dead man's inner organs, poems are born, mate, change and die.
The dead man's genitalia have caused him many problems.
When the dead man's writing is called "poetry," he laughs derisively.
The dead man sees no difference between a line and a sentence.
The dead man distributes definitions of poetry by reshaping the concept.
"Oh Dead Man, Dead Man," sings the nightingale of tradition.
"Dead Man, oh Dead Man," sing the masses of sparrows.
The dead man, like Keats, shall live among the English poets.
The dead man is perfected fallibility, the dead man shines without reflecting,
      the dead man is one of one, two of two, three of three, etc.

2. More About the Dead Man and His Poetry

When the dead man writes a poem worth preserving, he immediately burns it.
The dead man burns everything he writes, but pieces survive.
The fragment is more than the whole.
It takes its place among the apocrypha.
The dead man's poems are studied as if he were Aristotle and their subject
    catharsis.
For every book, there is one poem that sells it: a love poem or a life poem.
The dead man writes a poem to woo them in.
The dead man doesn't need to do life-writing. Oh windswept plains!
In the dead man's lexicon, a simple word for a thing, such as "tree," goes
    everywhere: its roots into history and prehistory, its branches into
    entropy and time, its leaves into beauty and belief.
The dead man looks into a cup of coffee and sees the plains of Africa, and of
    course his face appears too.
When he looks down, there appear to him, in the panel of such substance
    as his vision encloses, the matter and the matter-with, events and their
    nature, the beginnings of inertia and the end of momentum.
The entire world starts from the dead man's fingertips and from the front
    edges of his toes, and in all things possible there is a foreground right in
    front of his eyes.
The dead man refutes those who say they have nothing to say, no subject, no
    data, no right, no voice except they first dip their feet in the Ganges or
    tramp the Yukon.
The dead man sees the world in a grain of sand and feels it pass through his
    hands.
He is the unblinking mystic of fiber, fluid and gas.
No manifestation bypasses his bottomless hourglass.

The Book of the Dead Man (#11)

1. About the Dead Man and Medusa

When the dead man splays his arms and legs, he is a kind of Medusa.

Thinking himself Medusa, the dead man further splays his arms and legs.

Now he can shake it, toss it, now he can weave a seductive glamour into the
source of all feelings, a glamour known to roots and to certain eyeless
vermin of interiors.

The dead man knows the power of hair by its absence, hairy as he was at the
near edge of immortality while his fame kept growing.

The dead man uses the ingredients of cosmetic products made just for men.

He pares his nails in the background, just as Joyce, the elder statesman of
rainy statelessness, pictured the alienated artist after work.

He snips the little hairs from his nose and from inside the shells of his ears,
for the artist must be laid bare in a light easily diverted.

He wears the guarded fashions of loose clothing so that changes that might
offend—the loss of a limb or a sudden hollow in the chest—may go
undetected.

Mortal among immortals, the dead man can change you to stone.

2. More About the Dead Man and Medusa

The dead man mistakes his rounded shoulders for wings.

His shoulder blades suggesting wings, the dead man steals a peripheral
glance and shrugs, causing a breeze.

While the dead man's nails keep growing, the dead man has claws.

Once the dead man has lain in the earth long enough, he will have snakes
for hair.

Who could have guessed that the dead man was this much of a woman?

Who knows better the extraneous ripple of a long yawn?

In the theory of the dead man, nothing accounts for his maternity.

The dead man will not move out of harm's way, nor leave his children, he
repeatedly gives his life for them.

Who else may someday be beheaded by a sword made out of water and weed?

Mortal among immortals, the dead man strangles the moon in saliva.

Domed and tentacled, capped and limbed, the dead man resembles a
jellyfish.

Under his wig, the dead man's waxed skull belies the soft spot on a baby's
head that turns whosoever knows of it to mush.

The dead man speaks also for those who were turned into stone.

The Book of the Dead Man (#12)

1. About the Dead Man and Mirrors

The dead man is a receptacle for ideas, not images!

The dead man forgoes the illusory world of action for the natural state
of existence.

Hell, the dead man spits on the grotesqueries of artistic effort!

Orpheus, a notorious polyglot, couldn't go anywhere without looking over
his shoulder.

The dead man sings songs denied to Orpheus without looking back.

The dead man holds a mirror up to nature in which none of it can be seen
by whoever stands before it to look—well, of course!

This is the difference between the dead man and Orpheus.

The dead man wills his mirrors, his stickum stars, his window glass, his
brass kettle, his crystal wristwatch, his flashlight—all of it to Orpheus
whose days are dedicated to looking for himself.

The dead man is reflective, but you cannot find yourself in his eyes.

The dead man offers neither praise nor blame but permission to follow.

The dead man, outwardly calm, seethes with a wild enthusiasm.

The dead man's mirror shows the bones but omits the flesh.

The dead man has no use for the kind of mirror in which the moon can cut
his hand.

He presses a coin to the face of a mirror to see how deep the image goes
because he admires optical artifice.

2. More About the Dead Man and Mirrors

To the dead man, the surface of a lake is a window, not a mirror.

The dead man sees to the floor of the river where he watches carp and other bottom-feeders eat the darkness.

He cannot swim but sinks to the ocean floor and crawls while holding his breath.

When the dead man hovers over a cup of coffee, he sees the grounds and reads in their suspension a prediction of atomization.

In the eyes of another, the dead man sees a pathway to blameless dreams.

The dead man misses himself, it is true, but only in the abstract.

Hence, the dead man shows no mercy to mirrors, his visage suddenly appearing on the surface to those who run screaming from it.

To those who hated their parents, the dead man takes on the facial attributes of a father or mother and slyly infiltrates the space between the glass and its backing.

The dead man makes no distinction between smiles and wrinkles.

To the dead man, a mirror is a source, a reservoir of light waves extracted from a world of appearances in which a backward look may cause years of handsomely bad luck.

To the dead man, the world is prismatic: hence, the refraction of each element in the model, each number in the equation, each image, each statement, each crystalline midnight.

The Book of the Dead Man (#13)

1. About the Dead Man and Thunder

When the dead man hears thunder, he thinks someone is speaking.
Hearing the thunder, the dead man thinks he is being addressed.
He thinks he is being addressed because the sound contains heat and
      humidity—or groaning and salivation.
Isn't that always the way with passionate language—heat and humidity?
The dead man passes burning bushes and parting seas without inner
      trembling, nor does he smear his door with blood.
The dead man can only be rattled physically, never emotionally.
The dead man's neuroses cancel each other out like a floor of snakes.
He is the Zen of open doors, he exists in the zone of the selfless, he has
      visions and an ear for unusual music.
Now he can hear the swirling of blood beneath his heartbeat.
Now he can fall in love with leaves—with the looping lift and fall of love.
Naturally, the dead man is receptive, has his antennas out, perches on the
      edge of sensitivity to receive the most wanton prayer and the least
      orderly of wishes.
To the dead man, scared prayer isn't worth a damn.
The dead man erases the word for God to better understand divinity.
When nothing interferes, nothing interrupts, nothing sustains or concludes,
      then there's no need to separate doing from not-doing or to distribute
      the frequencies of the thunder into cause and effect.
The dead man speaks God's language.

2. More About the Dead Man and Thunder

The dead man counts the seconds between lightning and thunder to see
how far he is from God.
The dead man counts God among his confidants: they whisper.
The dead man hears the screams of roots being nibbled by rodents.
He notes the yelps of pebbles forced to maneuver and of boulders pinned
into submission.
He feels the frustration of bodily organs forced to be quiet.
He thinks it's no wonder the sky cries and growls when it can.
The dead man's words can be just consonants, they can be only vowels, they
can pile up behind his teeth like sagebrush on a fence or float like
paper ashes to the top of fathomless corridors, they can echo like wind
inside a skull or flee captivity like balloons that have met a nail.
The dead man serves an indeterminate sentence in an elastic cell.
He hears a voice in the thunder and sees a face in the lightning, and there's a
smell of solder at the junction of earth and sky.

The Book of the Dead Man (#14)

1. About the Dead Man and Government

Under Communism, the dead man's poems were passed around
    hand-to-hand.
The dead man's poems were dog-eared, positively, under Communism.
The dead man remembers Stalin finally strangling on verbs.
And the dead man's poems were mildewed from being hidden in basements
    under Fascism.
Embedded in the dead man is a picture of Mussolini hanging from a noun.
The dead man didn't know what to say first, after the oppression was lifted.
The green cast of mildew gave way to the brown stain of coffee upon coffee.
Suddenly, a pen was a pen and an alligator only an alligator.
A pig in boots was no longer a human being, a dead man was no longer
    alive though everyone knew better.
Now the dead man feels the steamy weight of the world.
He trembles at the press of the witch hunters, their clothes like night.
He has in his memory all tortures, genocides, trials and lockups.
He sees the lovers of pressed flowers brought down by botanical poverty.
He sees the moviegoers, who kissed through the credits, stunned by the
    sudden light after the ending.
In the lobby, the dead man's manuscripts went under coats and into pockets.
Then they all went off to spill coffee and argue ethics.
The dead man is the anarchist whose eyes look up through the bottom of
    the glass raised in toast.
The dead man is sweeter than life. Sweeter than life is the life of the dead man.

2. More About the Dead Man and Government

The dead man votes once for Abraham Lincoln, but that's it.
That's all he's time for (one man/one vote), so the dead man votes for
     Abe Lincoln.
The dead man votes with his feet, lashing his possessions to his back as if he
     were Ulysses tied to the mast to resist the siren call to stay put.
The dead man votes with a gun, disassembling it, beating the parts into
     scrap metal for farm implements.
The dead man votes with wet hands, a fishy smell lemon juice can't cut.
He comes in off the boat, off the farm, from the cash register and the time
     clock to throw down a ballot.
The dead man is there when the revolution stalls in a pile of young corpses.
It is the dead man's doing when the final tally is zero to zero.
The dead man is the freight man on the swing shift at the end of the line.
The dead man remembers the railroads run down by automobiles, the
     fields commandeered for storm sewers, the neighborhoods knifed
     by highways.
The dead man thinks a dead Lincoln is still better than the other candidates.
He knows that death stops nothing, and he hopes to be placed among
     the censored.
His immortality depends on the quality of his enemies.
He sees a wormy democracy spilling from the graveyards, its fists flailing at
     the target.
There is hope, there is still hope, there is always hope.
The dead man and his fellow dead are the buried treasure which will
     ransom the future.
You have only to believe in the past.

The Book of the Dead Man (#15)

1. About the Dead Man and Rigor Mortis

The dead man thinks his resolve has stiffened when the ground dries.
Feeling the upward flow of moisture, the dead man thinks his resolve
      has stiffened.
The dead man's will, will be done.
The dead man's backbone stretches from rung to rung, from here to
      tomorrow, from a fabricated twinge to virtual agony.
The dead man's disks along his spine are like stepping stones across a lake, the
      doctor told him "jelly doughnuts" when they ruptured, this is better.
The dead man's hernial groin is like a canvas bridge across a chasm, the
      doctor said "balloon" when they operated, this is better.
The dead man's toes are like sanded free forms and his heels are as smooth
      as the backs of new shoes, the doctor said "corns" when they ached,
      this is better.
The dead man's eyes are like tiny globes in water, continental geographies in
      microcosm, all the canyons are visible, now washed of random hairs that
      rooted, now free of the strangulated optics of retinal sense, this is better.
All the dead man's organs, his skin, muscles, tendons, arteries, veins, valves,
      networks, relays—the whole shebang hums like a quickly deserted
      hardware store.
To the dead man, a head of cabbage is a forerunner of nutrients.
The dead man's garden foreshadows the day it is to be plowed under,
      agriculture being one of the ancient Roman methods for burying the
      Classics, the other was war.
No one can argue with the dead man, he brooks no interference between
      the lightning and ground, his determination is legendary.

2. More About the Dead Man and Rigor Mortis

You think it's funny, the dead man being stiff?
You think it's an anatomically correct sexual joke?
You think it's easy, being petrified?
You think it's just one of those things, being turned to stone?
Who do you think turns the dead man to stone anyway?
Who do you think got the idea first?
You think it's got a future, this being dead?
You think it's in the cards, you think the thunder spoke?
You think he thought he was dead, or thought he fancied he was dead, or
      imagined he could think himself dead, or really knew he was dead?
You think he knew he knew?
You think it was predetermined?
You think when he stepped out of character he was different?
What the hell, what do you think?
You think it's funny, the way the dead man is like lightning, going straight
      into the ground?
You think it's hilarious, comedy upstanding, crackers to make sense of?

The Book of the Dead Man (#16)

1. The Dead Man's Debt to Harry Houdini

The dead man thinks himself invisible because of Harry Houdini.
Because of Harry Houdini, the dead man thinks himself invisible.
He thinks himself invisible because, who is to say he is not?
Because of Houdini, the dead man allowed himself to be placed in a box
    and the box nailed shut.
Because of Houdini, the dead man lay down after waving valiantly to
    the crowd.
Because of Houdini, because of Harry Houdini, the dead man holds
    his breath.
The dead man is like the apocryphal yogi, inhaling but once, exhaling at the
    door to eternity.
The dead man can whittle a bone into a key, he can braid rope from hair, he
    can pry open a crate with his still-increasing fingernails.
The dead man listens for a word agreed to by Mr. and Mrs. Houdini, never
    divulged, to be used to communicate from the beyond, a word that can
    slither upward, a word as damp and airy as the center of a soap bubble.
The dead man mistakes grace for worth, escape for thought, the past for the
    future, the sunken underworld for a raised stage, nonetheless the dead
    man will out.
The dead man thinks Houdini is a real Einstein.

2. More About the Dead Man's Debt to Harry Houdini

The dead man challenges the living to escape from his cuffs.

He accepts any challenge, any imprisonment, any confinement or stricture,
      any illness, any condition, and each time he lingers in the vise or jaws
      or jacket or cell before he chooses to appear again, always the picture
      of unrestricted beauty.

The dead man hides tools under a paste the color of his skin, his teeth are
      removable tools, he has seen the plans sketched in the dirt.

The dead man, like Houdini, is a locksmith by trade, a prisoner by vocation,
      an escapee by design.

The dead man has as many layers as an onion, as many tricks as there are
      trades, as many seeds as a melon, as many weathers as there are winds.

The dead man is dying to get out of tight situations using the technique
      of atomization.

The dead man may agree to lie in a frozen nest, to cling to a seashell rinsed of
      life, or to hang in the ether, but then the dreams come and he goes flying.

Like Houdini, the dead man has no intentions, only circumstances.

The dead man thinks Houdini the Einstein of escape artists, what with his
      youthful brilliance and his redefinition of the universe into here
      and hidden.

The dead man's broken wings deny gravity.

The Book of the Dead Man (#17)

1. About the Dead Man and Dreams

"Enough," says the dead man, grinding his teeth, checking his bite.

"Enough," the dead man says again, with his lips met loosely and his teeth apart so that the hum resonates, a choral trick.

The dead man's music-to-the-max, he has the diaphragm to sustain high notes, he has the embouchure to flutter and slur, he has the circular breathing to eliminate rests.

Hipsters, bohemians all gather fully themselves in mid-century past to hear the dead man blow.

There's jazz there, and the dead man spots the spilled coffee of poets rambunctious for Ionics, potters who pull from the inside out, painters of inverse volumes, sculptors freeing prisoners from stone, it's a time when plenty get it.

Getting it's the secret, ask the dead man, technique is epiphanic.

Upping the ante's the secret, ask the dead man, vision costs.

Swinging after midnight, grooving at 2, being hot or cool, knowing the body, indulging in a feisty surrender—ask the dead man, his secrets are out in the open.

The dead man disdains metabolic hooey.

The dead man is always in motion, like a pebble dropped into a lake, like a finger stuck into an eye, like a permanent wish.

The dead man sings and plays as well in sleep as awake, he positively trumpets down the walls of times past.

The dead man dreams of the intimate, animated toys of childhood, through which pass the pensive clouds of adolescence resembling things removed to a safe distance, and the icons of free logic: sad-eyed violins, ships navigating the equator inside bottles, messages written in lemon juice, screaming candles and such.

Whoever comes before the dead man for judgment, he shall be judged.

The dead man fingers the suspect, he has nothing to hide.

To the dead man, logic is the light inside the crystal, refracted, unavailable
    otherwise.
The dead man takes a hammer to a piece of coal to let out a diamond.
He squeezes an ornament at Christmas to reveal the blood that was inside.
He creases the water at flood stage, he shoulders the blame, he interrupts, he
    insists, he bends light.

2. More About the Dead Man and Dreams

To the dead man, North Dakota is in the closet.
The dead man makes no distinction between a map and a place.
The dead man is glued to existence, he is wishful and watchful but he
    doesn't need to know.
Things appear altered in his dreams: milk in black light, footwear
    rearranged by cubists, friends who talk out of both sides of their
    mouths like Egyptian figures seen from two sides.
If he could only have been white hair forever!
If he could have suffered indeterminately, seaweed tossed to and fro in sight
    of shore.
If he could have been a bottom-feeder without having had to die!
Achhh, the dead man has dreams within dreams, he has the claws to grip
    an altar, he rolls up the dirt, he plies the waves, he rides the wind, he
    crosses time lines without touching his watch, everything happens at
    the same time.
From the dead man's point of view, perspective is a function of time, not
    space, so to him a dream is a whistle to shatter the known frequencies.
The dead man drinks from a fractured goblet.

The Book of the Dead Man (#18)

1. The Dead Man's Advice

"Well, I wouldn't be so hurry if I was you."

The dead man starts with a wake, halbeit (sic) in salmon time.

"You don't know tunnel's end, but hell."

The dead man catches hisself pigeon-talking, neck over the moment unstill.

Like a pigeon, the dead man's iridescence aflutter.

Dead man carried aloft messages War-to-End-All-Wars, now extinct.

"What's rush, what's linger, neither of none's the one, where it ends."

"Who," the dead man, "wants to know?"

The dead man rubs the leatherette of his Dante, considering Hell.

He riffles the sheets of his Shakespeare, the revenge parts.

"You let *catharsis* out, you've got nothing."

"Your dreams mature, there's no childhood, best be dumb."

The dead man's got hokey and corny and the dwarfs of ideas that gambol in
    dreamland, that carnival tent, that circus of perpetual motion.

"I decent ideas crash and burn, sometime, Sometime."

The dead man sees the leaves sweat before they lose their umbilicals.

2. More Dead Man's Advice

Between a rock and a hard place, between sleeping and waking, between
      Gurdjieff and Ouspensky, among cattle and chattel—
Oh, the dead man goes straight.
Happenstance the location, circumlocution the path, the dead man towers.
"Unrapidly, you mean to get there, do you not?"
Oh the dead man, consent for resolutions, student of the betterment,
      refinisher, repairer, partaker of samples with the whole in mind—
Oh, how straight the dead man gone.
"You got blame to give out none, rightchyar?"
"Who," dead man, "there goes?" what with bearing wonderment.
"Kierkegaard, let's try," who proclaims laughter to be prayer, "what with his
      name lilting, that's something right off."
Having the requisites, lacing the particulars, bearing the burdens,
      tempestuous among frights and nights—
Oh, how slappy the dead man chokes time, Heimlich to make it talk.

The Book of the Dead Man (#19)

1. About the Dead Man and Winter

When the dead man's skin turns black and blue, he thinks it is winter.

In winter, the dead man gathers and insists, slipping his collective
    unconscious forward like a blue glacier.

When flowers turn under, he sees the stars blooming above, florid in their
    icy reaches.

When leaves desert the trees, he reads the calligraphy of the limbs.

The dead man endures material eternity with a shy smile.

The dead man in winter envelops, he encircles, he reaches around him like
    the possibility of wings on a butterfly.

In winter, the dead man tries on chaos in its fixed form.

His hollow deformity lasts and lasts, his shapely presence maintains the look
    it was given: that much longer is he gripped.

The dead man knows why the cherry tree waits for spring.

The dead man senses the earth going to sleep, he feels the vast organism
    within which he is a brainy parasite sputter and collapse.

The dead man waits with the bear in its cave and the rabbit in its hutch in
    the snow.

To reduce pain and swelling, the dead man takes six months of winter.

The dead man swallows winter, he applies it, he rubs it in, he wears it
    for support.

The dead man's head in winter lies like a cabbage in repose.

Under a blanket of dormant weeds, he basks in the brittle formality of the
    gray salon.

When there is no adversity, no rise and fall, no ascension, no decline, no
    frost too early, no season too soon, then there's no planet too unstable,
    no ship in the sky better than another for the journey of a lifetime.

The dead man's white flame is the last trace of ash.

The dead man through the scrawny stalks of beheaded weeds offers up the
    slightest scent of a place where live fish wait to be thawed and roots
    fall silent.

No one knows better than the dead man the chalk made from common
     materials that accretes around each organism deprived of water.
The dead man in winter is not just winter.

2. More About the Dead Man and Winter

The dead man in winter is the source of spring.
The dead man turns equally to all seasons with the cachet of a guest only
     momentarily served and all too soon departed.
What do you mean, not wiping the glass of the dead man's fingerprints?
What do you mean, disengaging from his small talk to rush to the side of
     fake heads of state?
The dead man freezes out the relentlessly glamorous, he does not welcome
     the vain nor host the proud, he turns from photos with too much hair
     and tilted heads, he absconds before the heat goes on in the bedroom.
To the dead man, all social gatherings are wintry.
To the dead man, a turn of the head leads to an ear full of dirt.
Oh winter, the season of warm hors d'oeuvres and cold counsel.
The dead man is the drumbeat of winter.
Among the frozen, among the polar thinking-caps and arctic questions,
     among the sled tracks and boot crevasses, among every poised paw
     print and running hoof mark, among the etched signatures of survival
     that everywhere mark the surface, the dead man models for eternity.
The dead man in winter is in heaven.

The Book of the Dead Man (#20)

1. About the Dead Man and Medicinal Purposes

The dead man's press makes a balm of beeswax.

He squeezes nectar from the orchid long folded into a book.

Where the dead man has found the strength to fix his grip tighter is a
sensuous mystery.

The dead weight of the dead man, you wouldn't think it, nonetheless hovers.

The dead man transcends gravity, clinging to the bottom of the earth, then
to the top, first one side then another, impervious to the siren call of
those frigid planets that patrol the heavens seeking the victims of black
holes.

The dead man's astronomy is to be taken with a spoonful of honey.

To the dead man, erosion is a form of CPR and an earthquake is the natural
consequence of the Heimlich maneuver writ large.

Writ large is the dead man's dosage of tranquilizers and antidepressants.

The dead man's remedy is to hold still, thus becoming a counterweight to
the hyperactivity of government and a counteragent to the passivity
of charity.

The dead man fights infection with the same alacrity he once used to effect
the peace.

When the dead man sank into the ground for good, a cease-fire prevailed
and nonviolence filled the void.

The dead man uses death and dying for medicinal purposes.

2. More About the Dead Man and Medicinal Purposes

When the dead man's fever breaks, he thinks the earth sweats.

Seeing the earth sweat, the dead man thinks his fever has broken.

The dead man suffers daily food poisoning from spoiled fish buried to
fertilize pines, rotted corn plowed under for lack of a price, wastewater
weighed by the ton, and countless variations of carbon whose days are
numbered seeping from landfills.

The dead man is in the path of sewage plumes, but a cemetery that large
cannot be moved.

Thus, the dead man must digest every chemical element to see what works.

In pain, the dead man puts repetitive phrases to an endless melody, he tries
gum and mints, he coats his stomach with pink oxides, but the tremolo
continues until he feels he will burst.

Now the dead man dines on mustard, now ferns, he swallows fungi
unselectively, he sponges up chlorophyll from cut grass.

When the dead man first turned his back and left, he felt green again.

When there is no attachment, no necessity, no need, no outcome, no
consequence of importance, then naturally sick is well, and the end
leads to a green beginning.

The dead man uses legitimate substances to break the law.

Like other living organisms, the cells and viruses that accumulate under free
enterprise visit upon the dead man.

The dead man catches cancer repeatedly.

Thus, the dead man reproaches Darwin's "survival of the fittest."

The condition of the dead man has been upgraded.

The Book of the Dead Man (#21)

1. About the Dead Man's Happiness

When the dead man hears the thunderous steps of an ant, he feels eager.

Sensing the reaching of a root, the dead man swells with metabolic anticipation.

The dead man loves the snoring of the sea and the absent-minded whistling of the wind.

He doesn't need much if it will rain now and then so that the weeds can flourish and a simple buttercup can get in position to sully a nose.

He likes listening to an ear of corn.

He loves the feeling of the wood when he drums his fingers.

He grows giddy at the thought of elk contesting and wolves patrolling.

The dead man does not choose sides between fact and fiction, night and day, beauty and truth, youth and age, or men and women.

The dead man can spend fifteen minutes opening and closing an umbrella, what a contraption!, its cone changes to a triangle and then a parabola, reordering geometry.

The dead man has turned his back on the planed edge of memory, each face from the past now bears the freshness of a cut orange.

The dead man's blood can be brought to a boil by a kiss, but also by dumb remarks about cows.

The dead man is an outsider by choice, unwilling to give up even so much as the graphite dunce cap of a wooden pencil and how it feels.

The dead man is one example, the rest to be filled in.

The dead man has it all, even the worms and the dogs.

2. More About the Dead Man's Happiness

The dead man wanted more until he had everything and wanted none of it.

At nerve's end, the dead man felt frayed and scattered: the profit-takers
wanted their share, and the bloodletters, the parasites, the actual
doctors, the patient embalmers, the donors, the grocers, the tailors, the
candymakers, and himself, too, lunging.

One day the dead man decided to keep himself as he was—sawtoothed,
tilted, uneven.

The dead man decided to stay short, lose his hair, wear glasses, get
heartburn, be pained, and thrill to his ignorance.

To the dead man, more mystery means more.

More fog, more vapors, more darkness, more distance, more time, more
absence—to the dead man, all is everything.

Put it down to the dead man's love of the watery rays of starlight.

Put it down to the dead man's lamentations.

One day something in the dead man rose from his body with a creak.

Under blank retinal covers he felt himself fill with happiness.

When he saw that he had displaced his weight in water, Archimedes cried,
"Eureka!"

The dead man did the same with substance and shadow.

The Book of the Dead Man (#22)

1. About the Dead Man and Money

Strange to say it, but the dead man needs sleep.

The dead man comes from a long line of people who had to make a living.

Therefore the dead man invests in futures: he eats.

He has working papers, he sells short and lives long, he leverages and
    hedges, he is himself a product of the gross national effort.

The dead man follows a money trail like an embolus on the long trek to
    the brain.

Who but the dead man foresaw the collapses of October, March, September,
    April, December, February, November, January, May, June, July and
    August?

The dead man's ledger is red for "ought"-this and "ought"-that, but he
    counsels not, lest he become the box turtle that tried to race.

His lips tremble with the good advice he withholds.

His knees quiver with the thought that he might someday move.

The thought of making a million sucks his brain dry.

Everything about the dead man's situation suggests no-load mutuals.

The weight of money makes the skin beneath his eyes sag.

The press of dollars gives him a thick pain in the chest.

His bones are edging away from the spidery fibers of hundred-dollar bills
    loosed from the pockets of burial jackets.

Inside the dead man's nose there lingers the odor of clean currency, a minty
    smell of ink.

Between the dead man's ears is the noise of hands riffling a wad of bills.

The dead man's eyes have a greenish tint, on his tongue there remains the
    residue of a rich dessert, and his skin has the texture of shredded
    excelsior.

Strange to say, the dead man is like a plate passed among the faithful, and
    the dead man needs sleep.

2. More About the Dead Man and Money

The dead man made a living—an outpouring of roses at the end.

The dead man made a living—the swaying of poplars by the sea.

The dead man is not blinded by the flare of economic downturns, nor
    deafened by boom times.

The dead man sees through the whitewash on the floor of the
    slaughterhouse.

The dead man hears the blood run backwards when the boss stands.

He knows the red mist in the eyes of the cutters when the whistle blows.

The dead man made bread and moola, a wage and a bonus, greenbacks
    and lucre.

The dead man, like you, fell from the branch when the season had ended.

The dead man, like you, lay underfoot as the pickers passed.

Like you, the dead man went up a tree into the clouds and cut it.

Like you, the dead man was nearly yanked overboard by a net full of fish.

Like you, the dead man, buying and selling, was bought and sold.

The dead man pays cash, he rates each and every economic ingredient
    beginning with the baker and his dough.

The dead man is certified, bonded, obliged, indebted and exposed.

The dead man's insolvency is a rush of water from a hole in Hoover Dam.

His deposits are earth, air, fire, water and time, which he draws by the lungful.

The dead man is legal tender, solid as a rock, good as gold.

By his will, the dead man disgorges his riches and turns *caveat emptor* on
    its head.

The dead man keeps no accounts.

The Book of the Dead Man (#23)

1. About the Dead Man and His Masks

When the dead man thinks himself exposed, he puts on a mask.

Thinking himself exposed, the dead man puts on a mask.

Before he needed a mask, he wore his medals on his chest and his heart on
his sleeve.

The dead man wears the mask of tomfoolery, the mask of assimilation, the
mask of erasure, the scarred mask, the teen mask, the mask with the
built-in *oh*, the laughing mask, the crying mask, the secretive mask,
the telltale mask, and of course the death mask.

The dead man's masks are as multifarious as the wiles of a spider left to work
in the bushes.

To the dead man, a spider's web is also a mask, and he wears it.

The trail of a slug is a mask, and the vapors from underground fires are a
mask, and the dead light of sunset is a mask, and the dead man wears
each of them.

The dead man curtained off the world, now everything between them is
a mask.

He weaves masks of sand and smoke, of refracted light and empty water.

The dead man takes what the world discards: hair and bones, urine and
blood, ashes and sewage.

The dead man, reconstituted, will not stay buried, reappearing in disguises
that fool no one yet cast doubt.

He comes to the party wearing the face of this one or that one, scattering the
shadows as he enters.

When there is no one face, no two faces, no fragility of disposition, no
anticipation, no revelation at midnight, then naturally years pass
without anyone guessing the identity of the dead man.

It is no longer known if the dead man was at the funeral.

2. More About the Dead Man and His Masks

The dead man's mask prefigures all *isms* such as surrealism, patriotism, cronyism, futurism, Darwinism, barbarism, Dadaism, Catholicism, Judaism, etc.

Many of the dead man's masks are museum pieces: final expressions from Death Row, those startled at the last second in Pompeii or Dresden or Hiroshima, faces surprised in the trenches, the terror of furnaces and lime, a look formed from suffocation or lengthy bleeding or embalming.

The dead man apologizes for leaving a sewing machine and an umbrella on the operating table.

The dead man catalogues war memorials, potter's fields, he takes stock of undiscovered suicides, pseudonyms and all instances of anonymity.

The dead man's masks are composed of incongruous materials accidentally combined and are as rare and wild as certain edible fungi that closely resemble poisonous mushrooms.

He doffs his hat to long hair, moustaches and beards, but does not give himself away.

He greets the grieving, the relieved, the startled, the victimized and the triumphant without letting on.

The dead man's hands are twice as expressive in gloves, his feet deprived of their arches gain momentum in shoes, and his mask shields him from those who wish to trade knowledge for truth.

The dead man's first mask was a hand over his mouth.

The Book of the Dead Man (#24)

1. About the Dead Man's Not Sleeping

The dead man squirms under a cow-jumped-over-the-moon moon.
Under a moon like the one the cow jumped over, the dead man squirms.
He squirms because he remains a child who can't sit still, who stays up
     nights until his brain has been wiped clean and his eyes are dry.
He starts over, the dead man does, as a child begins each day.
The dead man in the morning is fresh as a daisy, pure as the driven snow,
     crisp as a new dollar bill, and he smells like a baby.
The dead man in the afternoon is as dull as dun dirt, he is passive, digestive
     and ruminative.
The dead man in the evening rummages toward midnight.
After twelve, in the a.m., then the dead man's lucent eyes look inward,
     focusing and amplifying the dark to a black hole in a skull.
The dead man is absolutely animal.
Hence, the unmoving dead man stores up energy to such a high voltage that
     it can freeze you to him.
Hence, the dead man when active tingles with escaping protons.
When there is no balance, no even or uneven, no regulation, no permissible
     range, no parallax, no one sunrise, then naturally the dead man from a
     little salt on his tongue may concoct a new perspective.
The dead man sees himself hanging from the hook of the quarter moon.
He watches himself touch his toes around the circumference of the whole
     moon.
Like the moon, the dead man's true face is in shadow.
Like the sun and moon, the dead man's visage is mistaken for a forward-
     facing attitude.
The dead man's positive portrait masks the necessary negative, the flatbed of
     minuses that leads a charge to ground.

2. More About the Dead Man's Not Sleeping

The dead man's blood rises and falls with the days: Monday, Tuesday,
   Duende, Wednesday, Thursday, Friday, *Duende,* Saturday, *Duende,*
   Sunday, *Duende . . .*
Within him mix the essences of all cultures: *duende,* soul, *joie de vivre . . .*
The dead man sorts through pure substances to concoct impurities.
To the dead man, all ingredients are at hand, every division and subdivision
   of matter, each flavor, each scent of intention—all at the bottom of the
   bowl, the outcome undeclared.
The dead man's bones are skeleton keys to history.
Only the dead man can unlock the past.
He is the neutral observer, the truce force, the peacekeeping mission.
His nonviolence belies his years, his pacifism seems an edgy avoidance
   when we look through our eyes instead of his.
The dead man will keep his word but he will not sanctify it.
In the moaning grass, the dead man hears a vernacular for all time.
The dead man's teleology is the busybody seesaw of an adult.
The dead man's Zen is the zero before numbers, a face of stone, the child
   before the man.
Hurry to see the dead man shining with a hidden light.
Go quickly to witness the dead man deepening with time.
The dead man lives while others sleep.
He whirls in the darkness, a faint blur in a wide field of night, an
   underground voice trying to soften the blows.
The dead man short-circuits infinity to bring life to the eyes of cattle.

The Book of the Dead Man (#25)

1. About the Dead Man and Sin

The dead man's brain has undergone metaphysical surgery.

The dead man can only know what he knows, think what he thinks, and feel what he feels.

To the dead man, a sin is a small bird and many sins are many birds.

The dead man thinks vice is like dust or sand, something blown about.

The dead man's civilization looks the same in ruins, same things underneath the foundation, same things in the air around it, same indirection of swirling currents.

The dead man thinks rectitude a pile of small stones that keeps something in place.

To the dead man, rigor is the discipline of exchanging atom for atom.

It's the same story when the dead man meditates on anything at all.

A small bird is one of something that comes down in bunches.

A large bird is a universe, an entirety held from above.

Intentions keep things in place, and change is a material flip-flop, a swap.

The dead man believes the evidence at the ends of his fingers: a misstep.

The dead man takes his direction from the placement of his feet, convinced that a pair of anything is no accident.

The dead man feels the tractor turning up the dirt and the soil reassembling in the grave.

The dead man hears the anchor descend in judgment.

He feels the waves sneer at the boat they break apart.

He senses the confidence of the rain in going where it wants to, and the condescension of the sun as it recalls.

The dead man is privy to mistakes, the mixed flock, the broken shadow, the indefinite article of faith, the powerless totem, the broken altar, the stopped prayer wheel.

The dead man's fiercest teeth were reborn as dust.

The dead man mixes with those in black suits to hear who judges.

2. More About the Dead Man and Sin

When the dead man finds a coin, he wants it to be heads-up.

Before he picks up a penny, the dead man wants it to be heads-up.

The dead man's good luck is a weapon to vanquish dragons.

The dead man has seen dragons of such cosmetic skill that their scent alone
    flattered the willows into a fatal swoon.

He watches for the horrible bird feet, the feverish tongue, the armored
    complexion.

After many encampments, the lamps are tepid in the dead man's vigil.

The dead man has it in him to hold still, to abstain, to decline.

When there is no more luck, no far side to a hard edge, no final rain, no
    fatal dehydration, no unwelcome visitation, no lingering suspicion, no
    terminal judgment, then the dead man is all black cats and rabbit paws.

The dead man is marked by night-walking on the grass, by the crisscrossing
    of predator and prey and the celebrity pedestrian.

The screech of a bird is like a whining keel in the darkness.

The dead man feels the earth nod yes and no with the legacy of the
    righteous and the tide of battle.

The dead man does nothing with the proof at hand or the direction
    underfoot, neither does he long for an edge to his neutrality.

The dead man's good deeds are ever bearing fruit.

The Book of the Dead Man (#26)

1. About the Dead Man and His Cortege

Dead man says "cortege" because, who knows?, means to be watched from
a distance.
In dreams lost, the dead man unquestionably meant something.
Just as well the dead man's language not in the dictionary, good outcome.
When there is no more approval, no okay, nothing sufficient or appropriate,
then it's just as well the dead man's words can't be looked up.
The dead man inclines toward an erasable slate.
The dead man knows what Hobbes said and goes along from Hobbes'
perspective: "nasty, brutish, and short."
The dead man holds to the horizon, the cause of perspective.
The dead man, not able to hold a pen to render, thus not having to decide
this side or that, doesn't see things Hobbes' way unless he tries to.
The dead man thinks Hobbes was one of those grass-is-always-greener
fellows who went into the jungle.
The dead man is a preservationist, a nutrition conservative, an inactive
environmentalist rotting within the system.
The dead man's cortege follows him for philosophical reasons, the students
of supernal gravity.
The dead man makes no tracts, leaves no artifacts not in fragments.
The dead man's skin no good for bookbinding, too wrinkled.
The dead man's eyes no good for marbles, out-of-round.
The dead man's ears no sound-system, scattered parts for a horseshoeing.
The dead man's bones skewer the architecture.
The dead man's veins and arteries no good for plumbing, stripped threads
and leaky.
The dead man's bladder won't hold air, so no balloon, no bellows.
The dead man's nails a poor mica, the dead man's hair bad straw.
The dead man's vocal cords no harp for a fork, won't hold a tuning.
The dead man's blood no good for oil, too much iron.
The dead man's shoulders a faulty yoke, ill-fit to the oxen.

2. More About the Dead Man and His Cortege

Drying, the dead man rises at dawn like active yeast.

At sundown, the dead man descends from that chemical pride for which
   body heat is the catalyst into the rag-and-wood vat.

The dead man is the chief ingredient in paper and in marks on paper.

Muddy blood is the ink in the leaves of grass.

The dead man's a craftsman of ivy, vines and the broken lattice.

The dead man testifies to wind, torn bushes and the clatter from the
   henhouse.

Placing the dead man is difficult, putting him away takes time, he knocks on
   the walls of a resonant cavity underfoot.

The dead man reappears by first light and last light, in olive light, in queer
   violet light, in blossoming light, defenseless light, torn light, frozen
   light, sweating light, and he himself is lit from within.

The dead man has the luminescence of rotting wood.

When there is nowhere to go to find him, no circumstance, no situation, no
   jewel in the crown, no gem of the ocean, no pearl of the Antilles, no
   map, no buried treasure, only woods and more woods, then suddenly
   he will appear to you with a cortege of wolves or foxes in the midst of
   your blues.

The dead man lives on Socratic dialogue and fungi.

The dead man has plenty of company.

The Book of the Dead Man (#27)

1. About the Dead Man and *The Book of the Dead Man*

The dead man thinks he is hungry when he hears his stomach rumble.
Hearing his stomach rumble, the dead man thinks he is hungry.
He thinks himself hungry because he doesn't think he is no one.
The dead man repairs to his study to eat his words.
He lingers to watch the hourglass change from time to no-time.
He leans at the window to look for whitecaps, thunderclouds, the accruing
      ozone of a low, the yellow cast of tornado air.
The dead man's bones are freezing, though his skin is room temperature.
The dead man's nerves will not give up, his tongue refuses to quit, his brain
      saves up until it sparks, his blood abandons his extremities to go where
      needed, his pulse suddenly races, even his eyes lean out to feel before
      they see.
Now his hands fly about to put-his-finger-on.
Now he beats himself about the shoulders to fix his yoke in place.
Now he sinks into the soil, now he ploughs, now he rips away the artificial
      crops to roll about in the glowing fungi.
In his study, in his box, in his prison, in his socks, the dead man returns to
      the land from which he was raised.
The dead man bought the farm, his number was up, he was supposed to be
      done for, he had reached the end of the trail.
The dead man lives on hunger because, what is more filling?

2. More About the Dead Man and *The Book of the Dead Man*

The dead man thinks he is satisfied when he is satiated, a mistake.

He thinks himself fulfilled when he is no longer hungry, an error.

Now his eyeballs burn, his skull leaks, and his skin pales upwards from
his wrists.

Now the words—first words, last words—come to life on their own.

Here is "insect," the truly meek of the earth, inheriting the ink.

Here is "vinegar," the aftertaste of pleasure, soaking into the paper.

Here are "bones" and "love" getting together, and minerals ride on the light
from stars.

The dead man wears a watch cap to the lobes of his ears.

He yanks on his sleeves and unrolls the tattered bottom of his sweatshirt.

His fever has broken that was induced, and the sweat dries with thermal fury.

All that remains is *The Book of the Book of the Dead Man*.

Valéry, a terminal idealist, abandoned the ideal.

There is a moment when the dead man, too, cancels further revision of
the impure.

Thus, the dead man is a postscript to closure.

The dead man is also a form of circular reasoning, the resident tautologist in
an oval universe that is robin's-egg-blue to future generations.

The Book of the Dead Man (#28)

1. About the Dead Man and the Continuum

Music stirs the dead man to nostalgia, he bubbles, he ferments.

Under music, the dead man reflexively labors to bear the past.

His liver shrinks, expelling the speckled sludge of diners and taverns.

His spleen sweats off a gray aura of languorous melancholia.

Dotted half notes and whole notes squeeze phlegmatically from the dead
man's windpipe.

The dead man's bones break new ground in solid geometry.

His blood vessels decant greenish oxides, a lifetime residue of electrolytic
conversion.

Every element disengages, every sinew unwinds, each organ tries to start up
to name a tune or recall a face.

The dead man can't say enough about particular purples, maybe woolen,
maybe hair dye, all twilights.

He won't come in out of the rain, he loves the outdoors because of what
happened there.

The dead man sleeps with his eyes open, so eager is he to catch a glimpse.

He hopes to keep time in place by wearing a run-down watch.

He attempts to stop the iron filings from lining up after the magnet has
been moved.

He tries to trick the compass by turning quickly, he diverts the wind, he
downshifts to mock the continuum with herky-jerky movements.

The dead man is the funster of metamathematics and metaphysics.

The dead man has perfected perpetual motion in the form of constant
gravity.

The dead man, in the company of all sentient beings, is on his way home to
the sun.

To the dead man, body heat is something to die for.

2. More About the Dead Man and the Continuum

Like Rip van Winkle, the dead man is not dead, he is just sleeping.

When the dead man's eyes flutter, it is twenty years earlier.

He thinks the stuff that comes through the food tube won't be fully cooked
for two decades.

He believes that the nuclear waste around him is beginning to glow.

He sees the toxins leaching through the canisters, and the purified water
leaking from the survival barrels.

The dead man takes the future with a grain of salt.

He bundles himself in contaminated rootwork, donating what he can to the
chlorophyll factories.

He flings himself on the timed-release capsules to keep the earth drug free.

Rip van Winkle survived through indolence and woke in the future.

The Hudson was thicker than he remembered, and it carried him back.

When there is no clear water, no river for the first time, no river twice the
same, no sure path to the sea, no cloudless mirror, then the stationary
dead man is a world traveler.

The dead man, circling in a rowboat or lounging on the dock, could see
ahead of him.

Time was, the dead man could see his face on the bottom.

The Book of the Dead Man (#29)

1. About the Dead Man and Sex

The dead man lowers standards, ha ha, sinking, steadily sinking.
The dead man is jovial ha in the tide pool peaceful zzz among the tubers
    thoughtful uh uh in the basement ho ho creating humph humph the
    foundations of modern thought.
The dead man throws fuel on the fire.
The dead man throws in spoonerisms, being lone bonely, he gathers the
    wordless words, the articulation of knee jerks and other reflexive
    gestures, the spill of an orgasm.
He puts in the *whoosh,* the *ssss,* the *ahhh* and *oh oh oh.*
He is hot for the body, heaping moan on moan.
The dead man is the outcome of ecstasy, everyone knows it and wants more.
The dead man's lapidary but orgasmic, nothing new there.
The dead man is the depository of fixed form, the vault for a cool customer,
    safe harbor, still he loves the juiced up joining in the midst of love.
The dead man lets the clock expire to be there.
He is a sponge that never dries, absorbing the dark water.
Omigoodness, the dead man does things.

2. More About the Dead Man and Sex

The dead man speaks the lingo of sizzle, the grammar of quickened
      breathing, he states the obvious: more is more.
To the dead man, the new moon is a rounded promise of romance.
The dead man's wounded moon heals over each attempt to explore her and
      comes again to flirt in the dark.
The dead man's understanding of the moon goes well beyond her face.
It travels beyond her light side, reaching around blindly but with faith.
The dead man seeks the becalmed, the held, the immobilized in himself and
      sets it free.
Therefore the dead man studies the day sky to see the early moon.
He knows the moon is the better half of himself, that he is incomplete
      without her, and he cradles her on his brow as she rises.
All these things the dead man does and more.

The Book of the Dead Man (#30)

1. About the Dead Man's Late Nights

When the dead man cannot go to sleep, he squeezes blood from a stone.
Remember, the dead man is lapidary but orgasmic.
The dead man extracts blood, bile, semen, saliva, hair and teeth.
He weighs fillings and counts moles.
He takes a look at himself in two mirrors at once.
Front to back, side to side, top to bottom, the dead man is a matrix of
      handprints, stitches, whiskers, tiny volcanoes where vaccinations
      took, mineral deposits left to unclaimed salvage, congealed oil of an
      insufficient tolerance, wax and water.
There are many ways to look at the dead man but only one way to
      understand him.
The dead man can pass through a keyhole, the lens of an eye, the eye of a
      needle, walls that have neither doors nor windows.
He can disappear and reappear, he can summon feelings, he can get down
      on his knees, he can wave from afar, he can tie himself in knots, he can
      twist a thought or turn it over, he can count sheep, but sometimes he
      cannot go to sleep.
What then does he say when it's why not?
He says absolutely nothing, precisely nothing, eloquently nothing.
The dead man has dissolved the knot in which his tongue was tied.
Whereas formerly the dead man was sometimes beside himself, now he is one.
Whereas formerly the dead man cohered in the usual way, now he thinks
      dissolution is good for the soul, a form of sacramental undoing viewed
      through a prism, a kind of philosophic nakedness descending a staircase.
He wants to be awake at the very end.
So the dead man gets up at night to walk on glass.
He tumbles out of his sheets to consort with worms.
He holds back the hands of the clock, he squeezes the light in his fists, he
      runs in place like a man on a treadmill who has asked a doctor to tell
      him what to do.

2. More About the Dead Man's Late Nights

The dead man mistakes numbness for sleep.

He mistakes frostbite for the tingle of anticipation, a chill for fresh air, fever
      for lust.

He thinks he could throw a stone to kingdom come, but he is wrong.

He is used to being taken for granite, for a forehead of stars or a swath of
      matted grass.

But the dead man is more than the rivulets chiseled into the marker.

He is far more than the peaceful view at the downhill border, the floral
      entry, the serenity.

The dead man is the transparent reed that made music from thin air.

His life has been a die-hard joy beyond the sweep of starlight, he transcends
      the black hole, he has weight and specific gravity, he reflects, he is
      rained on.

The dead man does not live in a vacuum, he swallows air and its ill effects.

The dead man is rapt to stay the course, fervent for each spoke of the sun.

The dead man is mad to ride the wheel to the end of the circle.

The Book of the Dead Man (#31)

1. About the Dead Man and the Dead Man's Beloved

The dead man and his wife have an ongoing conversation, make that
　　discussion, let's say debate, call it a disputation, maybe it's an
　　argument.
To wit: who gets to go first, the dead man or the dead man's beloved?
When the dead man's wife strikes the dead man's funny bone, a kind of
　　electricity surges from his elbow to his pinky.
The dead man and his wife bump their skeletons together like keys in
　　a pocket.
When the dead man strikes his funny bone, his arm goes rubbery and his
　　pinky quivers like a ripe raspberry.
When the dead man and his wife bump their bones together, there's no
　　disputation, there's thesis and antithesis, action and reaction, give
　　and take, physics and geometry, but there's no discourse in any
　　metaphysical sense.
Notwithstanding literary compasses and other mathematical, magnetic or
　　gyroscopic conductors of sexual metaphor.
The dead man's funny voltage is all physical.
When the dead man comes, he goes, and when he rises, he falls.
The dead man is the only one who goes to the ends of the earth for his
　　beloved.
To wit: if they can't go together they aren't going at all.

2. More About the Dead Man and the Dead Man's Beloved

The dead man asks the lanterns to please whisper.

He asks the horses to whinny softly and to paw the earth gently.

He requests of the shovel that it move slowly in effecting its sharp separations.

He beseeches the dirt to be soap, the flowers to be fans in the heat, the
shadows to be blankets for the evening.

To the mourners, the dead man offers a shot of Frangelico in a cup of
steamed milk, he calls it a "split fountain," remember its name.

The dead man suggests a line or two after the ceremonial text, he calls it an
"aftergraph," it's beyond closure.

The dead man can light a match in the wind, he can open a bottle on a car
door, he has ways.

The dead man can rub his stomach and pat his head, he can make his arms
revolve in opposite directions, it's easy now to be akimbo.

What was so funny about the funny bone that the dead man cried out?

Who will win the argument in their sleep?

What was the word Houdini spoke from beyond, oh foil trumpets!

The dead man and his wife, being of one mind and frequently one body,
warrant that their fondest wishes have been granted.

Agreed to, this day of days, in this month of months and year of years, by the
undersigned, a.k.a. the dead man, the vouchsafer, the night custodian.

The dead man has bracelets in the skin on his wrists, rings engraved on his
fingers, and the ache of love in his bones.

When the dead man lies down with his wife, he breaks into a smile because
night tickles his fancy, strikes his funny bone and otherwise breaks
him up.

The Book of the Dead Man (#32)

1. About the Dead Man and the Apocalypse

When the dead man feels the heat, he thinks he's in the spotlight.

Engulfed by flame, the dead man thinks he's the center of attention.

The dead man rehearses the impending collision of Earth and the sun.

He hears the fly buzz and the snake retreat: sounds from the ebb and flow of
    global warming.

He feels the ivy wilt and the holly wither: victims of an intolerant
    greenhouse.

The dead man is perspective itself, the universal focused to a pinpoint, the
    microcosmic magnified to the power of uninsurable Acts of God.

The dead man is not the materialist but the material!

To the dead man, the melted paraffin of a candle is a slow-moving bog.

To the dead man, the rose petals are a tornado and the eulogy high tide.

Natural forces are all the dead man has or needs, he deduces, he intuits.

The dead man at the beginning is likewise at the end, he finishes what he starts.

Now come the sequential nights of retraction, when the dead man recants.

Darkness supports the dead man's reversions as the porous days did not.

Now the dead man hears what it must have been like to have started
    the world.

He loiters in the holes of astrophysical theories, likely at any moment to
    break through with a hypothetical work stoppage.

The dead man alone understands what it means to do less.

The dead man more than others has what it takes to make something
    from nothing.

Above all, the dead man takes inventory from scratch.

When there is no measure of candlepower sufficient to enlighten, no
    temperature, no tolerance, no voltage, no current, no draw, no output,
    then it's historical lunacy to throw off a moon.

Yet the dead man casts bread upon the waters, he throws caution to the winds.

When the dead man reaches the Void, he may throw an empty eyeball into
    space to start the whole thing up again.

2. More About the Dead Man and the Apocalypse

To have come to an impassable barrier, to have reached an unbridgeable
　　　chasm, to have come to a stitch in the fabric, to a peeling veneer, to
　　　know that under the stone is a city of slugs—
Before the birth of the dead man, it was not possible to return.
It was not possible, it was preconceptual, it was discretionary to the point of
　　　chaos, since of course there was nowhere yet to return to.
Since the birth of the dead man, however, it is even likely that one may
　　　return from the future.
The dead man walks ever more slowly into the past.
The dead man still has the upstanding bones of all the erect, but he no
　　　longer knows how to walk.
The dead man sits to walk, lies down to walk, crawls to walk, walks by
　　　mistake, by the skin of his teeth, by the seat of his pants.
It is easier for the dead man to pass through the eye of a needle than to ride
　　　a camel to paradise.
The dead man is the living Diaspora.
Say about the dead man that he took nothing with him but left it all.
The dead man's love for you is timeless and free.

The Book of the Dead Man (#33)

1. About the Dead Man and a Parallel Universe

Perhaps it is not so important that the dead man lives.

After all, the dead man deserts the future.

He squints to better define the distance, a darkroom procedure.

He drops his jaw to hear better, he makes a fist around each thing to gain a
    better purchase, he breathes with his mouth open to better catch the
    odors of food and inhales as he chews to better free its taste.

He walks downhill whenever possible.

Thus the dust where the dead man lies is fluffy, as if there were a shadow
    shape within it, a more perfect dead man.

Hence the face of the earth wears an expression of beneficent indifference,
    confirming that too much has been made of life and death.

The dead man will be tears freed of eyes, laughter and moans independent
    of any contraption, a soul without devices, a spirit sans tricks.

The dead man is Darwin's resolution, an ultimate promise.

After the dead man, how can there be a body of myth, he is the living truth.

The dead man seems smaller only because of where one stands to see him,
    this is mental parallax.

2. More About the Dead Man and a Parallel Universe

It is as if there were being woven a cloth shirt made of the fibers of dead
　　men, and of course it will be perfect.
People will take turns wearing it, each one imagining himself to be its owner.
A true knowledge of it will banish weariness and ennui.
The feel of it will be like solace in the rain, its wearer will shiver once and
　　once only.
To the dead man, the universe is a negative of a negative.
Thus, the dead man's minuses combine to form the pluses of a parallel
　　universe.
When the dead man's effects have been fully distributed, his entropy come
　　to fruition, then the imaginary numbers combine to pile up in reality,
　　denial is replaced with permission, safelights with daylight and the
　　fourth dimension with a greater three.
The dead man is over the top.

Ardor: The Book of the Dead Man, Volume 2

(1997)

> *For a long time pure linear painting drove me mad until I met Van Gogh, who painted neither lines nor shapes but inert things in nature as if they were having convulsions.*
>
> Artaud: "Van Gogh: The Man Suicided by Society"

> *To be at all—what is better than that?*
>
> Walt Whitman

Preface

The Dead Man is more alive for being alive and dead at the same time. Thus, the distance has narrowed between the known and the unmentionable. He disdains the hully-gully solemnity of ordinary grief and the torpid grin of groundless bliss. His is the body that is also the soul. That is, blood runs thicker than water, and the Dead Man is like bread for gravy.

The Dead Man knows who made love under the rising cloud of Vesuvius. The Dead Man was there when the Trojans fell for Helen. He knows that a stain in the earth may carry the genetic code for a lifetime of maladies, and he flings himself again and again on the ground to leave something to others. Things go, time goes, while the Dead Man stays.

The Dead Man is not a persona, not a mask. The Dead Man will not be organized by a box or a circle, a sign or a sum. His quantum, millennial presence-absence permits him to travel in the dark matter of space and in the sticky stuff of an atom.

Microscopics and macroscopics. Oddly transported.

It will be the absolute precision of the thing that undoes the thing. Likewise, our minds traveling any distance to the unseen rub up a fog and a static. Therefore, it is with no-mind, with perfected fallibility, with the fullest participation, and with no strings attached that the Dead Man ardently inhales the beginning and the end.

The Book of the Dead Man embraces life. It was written for whoever believes in the power of ideas to transcend the discrete, which is to say those who hazard philosophy and who believe also that an idea should have a little dirt on its shoes.

Dead Man poems were not intended to remain imprisoned as literature but to be useful without—a tool by which to meditate beyond conjecture. *The Book of the Dead Man* is but a basic work, fundamental. Let those who can make use of it excerpt and reshape it. Let those who can stand it, stand on it. As commentary, it welcomes more commentary. The Dead Man stands on the target, watching the world betray itself for a quiver of arrows. The Dead Man prefers to point his flashlight toward the stars.

M. B.

Ardor: The Book of the Dead Man, Volume 2

The Book of the Dead Man (#34)

1. About the Dead Man, Ashes and Dust

The dead man is slag ash soot cinders grime powder embers flakes chips
   slivers snippets lava and sand.
He is fumes fog smoke and vapor.
Do not mistake the exhausted dead man for the mangled, dissolved or
   atomized.
His mark is not a blemish on the earth but a rising tide of consciousness.
His tracks are not the footprints in the foyer but thoughts brought to bear.
The letter of the dead man impedes, but the letter and the spirit of the dead
   man together animate.
The dead man is not the end but the beginning.
To conceive of the dead man is the first act of birth, incipient.
The dead man was first.
At the table, nothing more can be poured into his empty bowl.
His is the whisper that cannot be traced, the hollow that cannot be leveled,
   the absolute, the groundless ideal, the pure—in all respects, the
   substance of the honorific.
That is, everything outside the dead man is now inside the dead man.

2. More About the Dead Man, Ashes and Dust

The dead man, Ladies and Gentlemen, clears his throat.

He adopts the rhetorical posture of one to whom things happen.

He rises, he appears, he seems to be, he is.

It is the dead man's turn to toast the living, his role to oversee the
   merriment, his part to invoke the spirits and calculate the dusk.

He is recondite in the dun evenings, deep in the sallow dawn, fit for
   contemplation all day, he is able to sit still, he lets his dreams simmer
   in the milky overcast of a day commonly pictured.

Who but the dead man has better drawn the covers over his head?

What better could the dead man have done to show his good will than to
   keep his secrets buried?

No one hath done as much.

Consider where the dead man goes at the end of the day.

Picture his brusque exits, reconsider his gruff respects, listen to his last
   words that found the nearest ear.

When the dead man clears his throat, it may be first words or last words.

When there is no birthday, no anniversary, no jubilee, no spree, no holiday,
   no one mass, meeting or service, then naturally it is up to each person
   whether to go ahead or turn back.

The dead man is 360 degrees of reasoning, three sides of a syllogism and
   four sides of a simple box.

The Book of the Dead Man (#35)

1. About the Dead Man and Childhood

In an evening of icicles, tree branches crackling as they break frozen sap, a
      gull's bark shattering on snow, the furnace turned down for the night,
      the corpse air without exits—here the dead man reenters his fever.
The paste held, that was dry and brittle.
The rotting rubber band stuck to the pack of playing cards to keep them
      together.
In the boy's room, the balsa balanced where there had once been glue.
Recognition kept its forms in and out of season.
Why not, then, this sweaty night of pursuit?
He has all of himself at his disposal.
He has every musical note, every word, though certain notes of the piano
      have evaporated.
Shall he hear them anyway?
The dead man's boyhood home withholds from its current occupants the
      meaning of desecration, nor shall they be the destroyers of the past in
      their own minds.
You too have seen anew the giant rooms of the little house in which you
      were a child.
You have seen the so-heavy door that now barely resists a light hand.
You have walked down the once endless corridors that now end abruptly.
Were you so small then that now you are in the way?
You too sat at the impossibly high kitchen table with your feet dangling,
      drawn down by the heavy shoes.
All this and more the dead man remembers the connective quality of.
In those days, there was neither here nor now, only there and the time it
      would take to reach it.

2. More About the Dead Man and Childhood

After Adam ate the apple, there was one more, and then one more . . .
After Orpheus looked back, there was another and another . . .
The dead man discerns betwixt and between, he knows mania and
  depression, he has within him the two that make one, the opposites
  that attract, the summer pain and the winter pain.
He walks both the road of excess and the least path, and lives most in the
  slow-to-ripen spring and extended autumn.
The dead man does not come when called but tries to hit a baseball in
  the dusk.
He does not yet know he wants to ride the horse that took the bit in its mouth.
He lives in the attic and the big closet where the radio parts and the extra
  glassware hold their codes.
He is the initiate.
He feigns nothing, he has nothing else in mind, later he will be charged with
  having been a boy.
Even now, in May and September he feels the throbbing tissue of that fallow
  world from which he was forced to be free.
The dead man in adulthood knows the other side, and he winces at the
  fragility of the old songbooks, taped and yellowed, held there in time.

The Book of the Dead Man (#36)

1. Drinking Glass, Pencil and Comb

This dead man's threesome is the true menagerie.

The dead man's menagerie represents the dead man's provisions, the
    expression and appearance of them.

When the dead man runs his finger up and down the teeth of a comb, it
    makes a zippy glissando.

An undercurrent of gnawing attends his ruminations because he chews
    his pencil.

The glass holds scissors, pens and pencils, a feather and other breakaway
    items.

If Socrates had never used a cup except to hold a few trinkets, the dead man
    would not now ponder the natural utility of objects.

If Diogenes had not carried a lantern, the dead man would not seek the
    genuine, the authentic and the valid in the bafflement of himself.

Oh, if there had been no pencil in the first place, no vessel, no tool of any
    sort, the dead man would not have had to travel by an oblique path to
    the end.

To gather, to say, to be shaped—in a glass, with a pencil, by a comb.

To speak or draw, to cough or *harumph*—the dead man designates forms of
    expression with and without words.

What has the dead man gathered in cups and vases, in bowls and glasses?

Do the missing teeth of his comb alter the musical scale?

Will the pencil have been fingerprinted, the graphite carbon-dated?

2. More About the Dead Man's Drinking Glass, Pencil and Comb

The dead man's comb shall fall from favor, his glass shall kiss another's lips,
     his pencils shall find other words to whisper.

The dead man holds up one hand to ward off the accidental collections, the
     detritus, the used-up but not discarded, but of course the world piles on.

The dead man as event, person or place is the leftover, the extra, the
     abundance too great for salvage, the too-much here and the little-
     enough there.

The dead man, like the Hundred Years' War, persists in the years following.

The dead man remains, like Diogenes' lantern, in the dark.

The dead man perseveres the way the Roman Empire keeps falling, with
     the music, the culture, the barbaric visitations, the evidence, the
     premonitions.

The dead man knows that each hemisphere of the brain acts in the light
     of conviction.

He has seen the contests of history: the insurgent peace, the one-sided
     negotiation, the unrecovered casualties, the tongue left in the goblet.

The dead man's relics are primitive by any standard.

The Book of the Dead Man (#37)

1. About the Dead Man and Little Much

High density sunshine adds weight to the dead man's eyelids.
Some say it's the humidity, but it's the heat.
The dead man, watching the surface percolate, charts the seepage.
It's the heat, it's the torpor of the day, it's the high cost of living.
The dead man is waysoever into lifting and living, what with pressure
     bearing down and the rushing about overhead to forget.
The dead man considers the greater good of the ne'er-do-well, the greater
     story never told, the seven sins, the seven wonders, the seven dwarfs,
     ancient expectations, previous versions, the discontinued, the
     remaindered, the deleted, the disappeared.
He, the dead man, being in fever and ardor, confirms that the frivolous is
     mixed up with the earnest, the make-believe with actuality, the old
     with the new, the living with the dead.
The dead man has littlemuch language for these precocious times.
What an era: the dead man poling for the bottom finds it fathomless.
For it was the nature of ethics to need language, however littlemuch.
The dead man has all the languages, the scripts, those based on sound, those
     based on picture, those based on interval, those soaked in adrenaline,
     those dry as English toast.
The dead man knows how hard it can be to speak with a mouthful of grit.
The dead man doesn't spit straight up.

2. More About the Dead Man and Little Much

It's little enough to be voiceless in a clamor.
The dead man shapes the din and the uproar, he puts potholes along the
      information superhighway, he blocks the ramps, he disconnects, he is
      offline, he interferes.
The dead man knows the roads and the music, the wires and the keys, are
      there only to make the rats run faster.
The dead man tries on one hat at a time, he is persistence of vision
      incarnate, he is knowing of the binary two-step, he is formidably
      with-it, he is hip but he knows better.
The promises of knowledge, this genetic free-for-all, these complete records,
      this Big Brother that has your number, this nonstop news,
      this access, this roundly thumped privacy—the dead man witnesses
      each incursion into the far reaches of ignorance.
He thinks at this rate the gauges will break and the computers crash.
He sees the sundials wobbling nervously over what time it is.
He sees the stars leaning.
To the dead man, nothing more is something else, a concept beyond
      population and resources, an idea whose time is past.
He has littlemuch lingo, littlemuch answers, littlemuch solar longevity.
Whereby the dead man rocks the planet to sleep, the song still on his lips,
      his covenant unbroken.

The Book of the Dead Man (#38)

1. About the Dead Man and Sap

The dead man will not add 1 + 1.

He squeezes things that settle near him until they drip a little.

The dead man's things shine with an oil pressed from the raw flakes of
      beached fish, the ripe carcasses of birds that winter would not release,
      the everyday jam and jelly of who wants what.

Who and the dead man have felt the earth heave though the air was still?

Who and the dead man have made their bed and lie in it?

It is a panoply, a plethora, a surplus, a surfeit, an abundance, a bounty and
      an earthly prosperity.

The dead man cut his hand caressing the scaled hearts of catfish and trout,
      he stiffened from gripping the back of the crab while its claws clicked,
      his joints display the geology of labor and lovemaking, he is wrinkled
      from laughter and stained from tears.

When there is no more wrinkling and weeping, no physiognomy of
      pleasure, no anticipation, no abundance, nothing extra, then okay it's
      the way it is, not the way we remember.

2. More About the Dead Man and Sap

The milk, juice and pitch of the dead man ebb and flow.
Lifting and falling, the dead man's inner ocean cleanses him of wanderlust,
    his days abroad now a ghostly apparition.
The dead man is fascinated by mirages, oases, missing tide pools, lost lakes,
    basins where rivers ran, wells that went dry.
He sees his face in the mud of a drained marsh.
The dead man does not plant his flag in the dust but doubles back like
    reflected light.
Pity naïve Narcissus, bent to a river that was moving on.
If there is a bit of froth, foam or lather, a few suds, an escaped bubble, a
    globule of blood anywhere, the dead man will find it and begin again.
The dead man finds it fortunate to have been in the train station when the
    coffin was loaded and the mourners toasted the departed who was
    just leaving.

The Book of the Dead Man (#39)

1. About the Dead Man and the Interior

When the dead man's arm goes numb, he thinks an emotion is leaving.

Feeling the loss of feeling, he thinks he feels less than he did before.

The dead man lived on whatever made him say *mmm* but now he'll exist less overtly.

Ashes are the dead man's contrition, dust is his handkerchief.

No, it's otherwise: contrite dust, handkerchief in ashes.

Some issues for the dead man: whether he is fish or reptile, whether he is milk or glue, how inadvertent his chemistry.

The dead man pulls the blanket up around his shoulders, then stretches a leg out to offer the cold a corridor inward.

He waits to see things the other way around: handkerchief turning to dust, contrition gone up in ashes, et cetera.

He observes the anniversary of the ushers when they come to replay their roles in the carriage of time.

Then the dead man was soft, but a year afterward he has been eaten away like an irradiated worry-stone.

The dead man's flesh, which blanketed all feelings, gives no further indication of his countless emotions.

All about the dead man, nickels collide with quarters and pennies with dimes.

For all who attended the dead man, none carries a key to the interior.

2. More About the Dead Man and the Interior

The dead man is the forked bearer of a swaddling cloth, many blankets, the
needlework of immunity and an ironed winding-sheet.

His Jew's-harp jawbone held the music in place.

His Semitic sternum contained that final heartbeat for which all preceding
heartbeats were a ceremonial preface.

When there is no more accidental, no inadvertence, no anthropological
terrain sufficiently confined, no chaos unlinked to further chaos, no
anarchy within anarchy, no thing of discrete substance, then nothing
may come between thought and feeling.

Why did the dead man believe he was losing feeling when all he was losing
was an uncontrollable shiver?

How was he supposed to know that the car was a coffin?

Why did the dead man step on the gas when the tank was empty?

The Book of the Dead Man (#40)

1. Socks, Soap and Handkerchief

The dead man is haunted by socks and soap.
Socks and handkerchiefs pile up in his cabinet and fill his thoughts.
The dead man wears away like socks in shoes or soap in water.
Dead man's soap has a windchill factor of room temperature.
Dead man's socks have holes in them where the toes went.
The dead man's handkerchief is a textbook in geometry.
What, to the dead man, means what, what with time passing muster?
The dead man twisted his wrist while trying to soap his back.
He sprained his ankles pulling up his socks.
He blew his brains out while using his handkerchief.
The dead man is feet-first, he is clean as wax, he is comforted.
The dead man wears socks on his hands to effect the look of mittens.

2. More About the Dead Man's Socks, Soap and Handkerchief

The dead man slid on soap, eased his way, stepped with care, wiped his
     glasses until they were too clear to see.
The dead man depends on his socks to match.
He loves to strip the wrapper from a bar of soap.
He puts himself through the wash-and-rinse cycles of the seasons.
He wipes and wipes the blades of his knife and repacks them.
The dead man feels loss, aging and grief—socks, soap and handkerchief.
He fulfills the expectations of maids, seamstresses and laundresses.
He sees the soaps replaced, the socks darned, the handkerchiefs refolded.
To the dead man, socks without holes are a sign of worldly cares.
To the dead man, soap follows the loss of innocence.
The dead man carries a handkerchief for show, for no reason, to have it to
     drop, to have it to pick up.
The dead man, gathering the used and lost, adds one more.

The Book of the Dead Man (#41)

1. About the Dead Man and Hot Topics

Reactive, resurgent, the dead man welcomes a steamy updraft.

Must all he's been amount to something?

What, going uphill, is the dead man's loftiest position?

Give him his organic druthers, his fleshy fast action, his dual feelings.

Let him lie down in your top spot, for he shall make its whereabouts known.

What was in the offing when, hearing his heart tick, the dead man
      wondered, Where truth and beauty?

Feeling his rib cage quiver, the dead man wondered, What thread, what
      stroke?

For he hath warred with the pebbles and the roots.

By turns, the dead man sprang upon himself, buoyed himself, suffered
      himself, sank within himself and rose from himself.

The dead man is intimate with grubs.

He sniffs the soggy earth, ingesting vapors of blood and semen.

The dead man bursts like spring in retaliation.

He endorses the behavior of the lower animals.

He cheers those who bed down on the pulpy forest floor and those who
      pursue their dreams.

Who more than the dead man savors the soft interior of an enigma?

The dead man, forced to live on abstract rations, chose love.

Was it God, or was it the wine?

The dead man, thumping within as if he might jump out of his skin, waits
      out the beats, outlasts the interval, all the time acting as if he were the
      lowest common denominator, the very one.

When there is no more regularity, no bottle of seeds, no injection of
      pollen, no gauze to map the outpouring, no tourniquet to staunch the
      expression, no crutch, no illness or health, then okay why not truth
      and beauty, why not blameless, helpless truth and beauty?

Tell me that, says the dead man, tell me, why not that?

2. More About the Dead Man and Hot Topics

The dead man has a bone to pick.

Gripping a wishbone, arming a slingshot, facing a fork in the road, the dead
man takes no sides, off in all directions, divergent from yes and no,
should and shouldn't, will and won't.

In his immersible dungeon, divining the shafts of waterways, calculating
time and tangent, the dead man relentless deploys his effects.

A piece of the dead man is down the road a piece.

Naturally, he will not vanish, naturally.

Nor will the dead man be delivered, he is habitually the remains.

The dead man's day heats up with the first glimpse of the familiar.

All is familiar to the dead man in the shimmering waterways of the
sun's fire.

All is wholly met by the dead man in the shining inferno of the tides.

Shall now his entire being stare into the fire, shall now he sit like a seashell,
shall now he tremble like a petal?

To the contrary, the dead man rises to shave the light layer by layer.

Few shall be given to fathom the dead man's passion.

The dead man frees his subjects—topical treatments fair in method and
random in result.

The dead man does not wince at the touch of time, nor does he finagle to
bring to light the compensations, tips and rewards, nor the grainy
gratifications that dissolve in unfixed emulsions.

When there is no more this and that, no indoors or out, no originals, no
effigies, no copycat lump of stone set to bang out the new universe,
nothing top or fancy, why then the dead man has all there is of
hot topics.

The dead man loves you because your brain kills him.

The Book of the Dead Man (#42)

1. About the Dead Man's Not Telling

The dead man encounters horrific conditions infused with beauty.

He looks and sees, dare you see with his unblinkered eyes.

He sniffs and ingests, dare you do the same as he.

He hears and feels, dare you secure such stimuli and endure the heart.

He sets foot on the anomalies, he traverses the interior laden with the screams of witnesses underfoot.

He walks among the pines crackling with the soon-to-be-broken backs of new life.

He freely rests among the appetites of the unsatisfied.

He bites off the head of the Buddha.

The dead man has seen bad Buddhahood.

He has doubled back, he has come around, he has cut across, he has taken the long shortcut.

What is out there, that germinates?

The dead man knows that there is no luck but dumb luck, no heart that will not skip, no pulse that does not race.

Things go, time goes, while the dead man stays.

2. More About the Dead Man's Not Telling

Has not the dead man asked a basic question?

Did he not lie in the crib like a question mark without a sentence?

Did he not encode the vitality of roots, the beauty of leaves, the kinetics
     of branches, the rapture of the sun, the solace of the moon, even the
     hollow that shapes the seed?

The dead man is the one to ask when there is asking.

Those who invest in the past or future shall forfeit the dead man's
     objectivity, his elasticity strung from down-and-dirty to up-and-ready.

When the oracle spoke, the dead man listened like a shell.

When the quixotic signaled from the wood, the dead man grasped the new
     life that needed no more plasma than the dew.

How comely the horrific consequences, how amiable the gorgeous
     advantage of the newly born.

Things go, time goes, but the dead man goes nowhere without you.

You who told him know what is on the dead man's mind.

You at the fringe, the margin, the edge, the border, the outpost, the
     periphery, the hinterland, you at the extremity, you at the last,
     counterpoised, have caught the inference.

The dead man counts by ones and is shy before your mildest adoration.

The Book of the Dead Man (#43)

1. About the Dead Man and Desire

When the dead man itches, he thinks he has picked up a splinter.

Unable to free himself of an itch, the dead man thinks he has a splinter.

The dead man looks at a praying mantis and sees a pair of tweezers.

He offers himself to be walked on by claws.

He waits for the odd fox to trot across his chest and strings of ants to scrape
     him pore to pore.

He anticipates the flaying action of chemicals and the sponge baths of
     the rain.

The dead man, scoured, is the ruby servant of the vineyard.

The dead man is the salt of the earth, the dust and the sawdust, the honey in
     the wine.

Hence, his thoughts must rise to the moon and beyond to take his mind
     from that splinter if it is a splinter, that itch if an itch is what it is.

Everything the dead man thinks has its other side.

The dead man thinks Saturn has been much married but forever lonely.

2. More About the Dead Man and Desire

If he were just valves and glue, just honey and chocolate, just hot and cold,
     the dead man's thoughts would not hop, skip and jump so.
If he were just comparative, if he were absolute, if he knew his own mind,
     the dead man's heart would not race so.
Who but the dead man wonders which of its moons Jupiter favors?
Who knows better than the dead man in his bones the pitch at which the
     earth breathes?
The dead man is rapt before the altar of consciousness.
He enters the forbidden realms of experience without penalty.
To the dead man, there is something grave about umbrellas, something
     sinister about servitude, something debilitating about knowledge—like
     sunlight on slugs.
The dead man rolls back into place the rock that was moved to find out.
Like Sisyphus, the dead man wants what he has.
When there is no more meek, no vainglorious, no catch-as-catch-can, no
     inheritance, no opportunity knocking that is not also the wind, then
     naturally the dead man lives for love.
The dead man, fervent to feel, makes no distinction between a splinter and a
     stinger that cost something its life.

The Book of the Dead Man (#44)

1. About the Dead Man and Humor

The dead man is very very laughing.

Why so whale of a jolly?

There's bustling and piercing that enticingly through the fabric of daily
    lives went.

There's old-style regimes that Communist went the way of, and Fascist
    repercussions the knowing of deserted and despaired.

Who from ancient times mystery has pondered, Latinate explosions in the
    postscript.

He doesn't care who knows, what with letters to be forged.

The dead man turned and rolled, the red thread he conjured.

The dead man came upon a tree and of a while carving it, was gentle but
    definite.

The letters he engraved there being grown now heatingly in the sun,
    exposure unruly.

What is fair?

All there he said was x loves y and why not?

The dead man very very laughing to be open and thought.

2. More About the Dead Man and Humor

Too hard to be the only survivor terrifies.
Too much to become hands-up not making a move just to get by.
Winds, stars, flags, masks—all defy, furthering.
The dead man can't say this or that, this being roundly rubber-banded to
    snap back, that too.
Into position the dead man takes up.
Wasn't lightning made the dead man glow, no flare-up suddenly.
Was unfleeting affection won him and gave him silly to be ofttimes when
    nothing accounted for it but she side-by-side.
The dead man apologizes for breaking training, wrenching syntax, turning
    topsy-turvy to be laughing down.
The dead man knows that beneath and below overhead come round.
The dead man, puffed and filled, scampers like a frantic wasp, his oath held
    back because the moment is coming.
He laughs to be knowing when knowing is laughing, with the punch line
    riding up just in time.

The Book of the Dead Man (#45)

1. About the Dead Man and the Great Blue Heron

When the dead man stands on one leg, he thinks he's a heron.

Wobbly, one foot out, the dead man thinks he's a heron but not a fish.

As a fish, the dead man knows he doesn't have a leg to stand on.

Still, fishpicker of cold waters, the dead man is off-and-on goofy, awhile whimsical or fitful, increasingly counter to the sparrow as which he first flew.

Naturalists of the dead man, who once recorded the sparrow's vigor and the exotica of the nightingale, now search the archaeopteryx's stone remains, seeking to foretell the strenuous operations of crane and cormorant, pelican and albatross.

The dead man, birder of pigeons and crows, mimic of warbler and whistler, favors in geezerhood the awkwardly limber, the footfall of the fragile shinbone, the critical exactitude of the next step.

What has happened to the dead man that he should turn sharply from the liquid beauty of dead nature?

Who now will mark the sea-change that swirls about him?

There's this about the dead man, that he can be more or less.

He is, more or less, the heron that met a loon.

Habitual, the proximate flocks took stock until nightfall.

2. More About the Dead Man and the Great Blue Heron

The dead man, rickety, compelled to wade the shallows with a hoarse croak
    for an anthem, still feels uplifted, transcendent, ecstatic, blessed,
    sanctified and generally okeydokey.
The dead man has been the bird of paradise, which is why.
Why is also because he has known the breeze that carries seed from
    the cottonwood in the spring and maple leaves from their sugary
    cupboards in the fall.
Therefore, from whatever he was, or thought he was, in whatever form
    faltering, it was there in the offing that fervor and peril would walk
    together, burrow, swim and fly.
When there is no one body, no two bodies, no bird that was not a fish, no
    fish that will not hover, no snake that cannot learn to walk, no man or
    woman who did not crawl, then the possible and the probable conjoin
    to grant the blue heron a step.
The dead man's golden eye reconnoiters fear and far, as he folds in his neck
    to try flight.
With his neck-stretch and wingspan, the dead man will reach the boundary
    waters of sense and apparition, all beneath an infinite sky.
Why is the dead man transfixed by birds come to earth and the great blue
    heron stilled by a wee trembling in the current?
Is it the goose bumps, is it the chill?
Why is because he is dizzy, not daft.

The Book of the Dead Man (#46)

1. About the Dead Man's Dog

The dead man, *that* man, consorted with canines in the turmoil of a
derangement sensed by few others.

The mongrel was apt, the mutt, the half-breed is best, the hybrid, the
mixture—being those of an underclass to which the dead man belongs.

The dead man's dog is immediate, primary, without tedious human
calculation.

The dead man's dog follows his nose, his tongue lags but accompanies, his
owner's voice mixes with the sighing of the browning leaves.

The dead man's dog is housebroken, barnbroken, fieldbroken, lawnbroken
but is free to go.

The dead man's dog keeps a tight leash on his master, dragging him to every
clandestine murmur, every rumor of affection.

The dead man's dog has the wherewithal to violate those senseless codes
meant to make a man or woman stay.

To the contrary, the dead man's dog shakes hands, he fetches, he heels, also
he behaves and misbehaves in human proportions.

The dead man's dog plays dead.

2. More About the Dead Man's Dog

When there is no more approbation, no license, no all-time immunity, no
    obedience or disregard, no loyalty that is not also the pick of the litter, no
    luck but dumb luck then okay it's not a show, and spunk is what it takes.
It takes the dead man an eternity to romp, meanwhile he learns a mutt's
    moxie.
Oh pretty dogs that reap the rage of benefactors in good times.
Oh dogs shorn of the outdoors, oh clipped, oh shaggy shaggy shaggy.
The dead man's dog does not sit up and beg.
The dead man's dog is the hybrid of now and later, bred to be good with
    children, eager, vigilant.
Hound and buddy, enthusiast of dishes and scraps, perch for fleas, station of
    sanity, trained to disobey in the nick of time—the dead man's dog runs
    beyond reason.
His is the virtue of the undersides of logs.
He readies his bones for the passage to the underworld.
He rolls before the fireplace, the whole house his sarcophagus, his face lit
    like that of an Egyptian jackal.
The dead man's dog's teeth are nine-tenths of the law.
His claws are the quills whose marks will be the stuff of history.
His tail is a brush for which the wide day is his canvas.
Eagerly, the dead man lies down with dogs, observer of puppy love and
    dog song.
The dead man's dog is a little bit of all right, a wagging yes, a cause of
    whistling and waving, cupped hands and come-when-called.
He bestirs the dead man's fortitude.

The Book of the Dead Man (#47)

1. Toaster, Kettle and Breadboard

The dead man lives in the flesh, in memory, in absentia, in fact and fiction,
     by chance and by nature.
What are we to make of his continuous use of everyday objects?
For the dead man's fingerprints are everywhere: his crumbs, his residue, the
     marks his tools made.
The dead man corks and uncorks the passable wine.
He needles the bad meat to make it tender, he breads the wings of the
     chicken, he takes from the incendiary oven his meal at leisure.
The dead man has no stomach for ordinary indigestion.

2. More About the Dead Man's Toaster, Kettle and Breadboard

The dead man sees fireweed grow from scorched ground.

He sees the conspicuous consumption of Thoreau, the torch-bearing saviors
  of Walden.

He reckons up the passionate aesthetics devoid of the smell of ashes.

He notes the footprints on the rice paper of those who seek divine
  abstinence.

He records and distributes the knowledge of fair game.

Did the dead man eat roasted bread or drink from boiling water or take a
  piece of something, leaving the rest?

There is only the evidence of the dead man's estate.

There is only the proof of toaster, kettle and breadboard.

The dead man does not confuse plain water with weak tea or piety with
  indifference.

When there is no more appetite, no inhalation, no absorption, no osmosis,
  no digestion, then okay let the reverie commence in the ether.

The dead man lives in the meantime, the in-between time, the time it takes
  to boil, broil, bake and fry, assimilating the cooked and the raw, the
  beefy and the lean.

The dead man is himself an ample morsel-to-be, a tidbit, a sweetmeat, slices
  and scraps and a mouthful of quills.

The Book of the Dead Man (#48)

1. About the Dead Man and Diminishment

Haply, the dead man has been reduced to the basics.

The diminution of a lifetime gives the dead man a way out.

Through the rafters of the trees there comes now a gentle buzzing, a shy
      laughter, a faint murmur expressing the apathy of time.

To the dead man, antiquity is a law unto itself.

It is scored in the creases of palms and inscribed but faintly on the
      undersides of eyelids.

The dead man merely mimics the modern affectation in being "positively
      medieval" about the fifth to fifteenth centuries.

The dead man knows that the buzzing is that of houseflies, not honeybees.

He understands the futility of the field mouse and the laughter of the owl.

He gauges the flight of the swift and the piecework of the predator.

For the dead man is the wizard of divination by the footpath of the crosses.

The dead man is tucked in to ride out the epoch.

He is the long and short of it, the more or less of it, the changes that were
      thought to be doomsday.

Beneath his fingernails is the debris of torches that were said to hold eternal
      flames.

The dead man had the last straw thrown down upon him innumerable times
      until he took the lot of it back to wheat.

He is the decaying cellulose and the throngs of microorganisms that desert it.

His is the saliva that ate away the rafters, the nails, the gadgets, the dingbats
      and the blueprints.

For the dead man is alternative, the possible reassembled as a hollow
      sphere in which the bounce, sound and feel of it depend upon the
      emptiness within.

Small as he is, little as he was.

The dead man's reticence, reluctance and restraint are as lucrative to him as
      all the tea in China and have the same effect.

But the dead man is happy to be sleepy.

2. More About the Dead Man and Diminishment

After tea, the dead man traces his chronology as well as those early trade
      routes that were the outer, overt primitive versions of synthesis.
The dead man, after tea, relearns the inner topography of his eyelids.
Who is to say that sleep is not the hollow of his ruminations?
Who would deny the dead man his afternoon shut-eye?
The dead man dozes to relive his vigor and the fantastical torpor of rest.
He snoozes to recall the drowsy aftermath of pleasurable storms.
No one but the dead man knows how passionately he fought in the arenas of
      solace and consolation.
It means this to be the dead man, the tablets agree.
The dead man, knowing that things end, is elated to be eternal.
Hence, the dead man sponsors all quirks and whims because glory is fleeting.
Because glory is fleeting, he trespasses on authority with impunity.
The dead man dances on the graves of the dour and the overly manicured.
When there is no more large or little, no unmarked brow, no unmapped
      eyelid, no white page, nothing ill-fated or rebuked, then the dead man
      rivals the nine muses of antiquity in being the root cause.
Physically speaking, the dead man's fragments are neither litter nor shreds
      but hyperbolic segments of minute organic activities.
That is, the dead man is too pleased to have it known, too joyful to say why,
      too intense to sleep late.
What is that clamor, that din, that uproar, that racket, that "wisecrack giving
      itself away as outcry"?
Is the dead man flavored or preserved, is he seasoned or is he cured?
Supine, not dormant, the dead man is prone to florid events in the
      atmosphere.
In the valley of divine wizardry, by the footpath of the crosses, it is the dead
      man who reckons diminution in lieu of time.
Kook, weirdo, oddball, nut, the dead man's makeup is one-part matter to
      one-part essence.

The Book of the Dead Man (#49)

1. About the Dead Man and the Elusive

The dead man has not and, having not, has.

Why anyone cannot see this is anyone's guess.

The organist who said "dead man, dead man, dead man" again and again, trying to expel it.

The man who wrote on the leaf of a gingko, "Here is death," as if it were necessary to die to be green again, and it is.

The man who evaded and consigned, the woman who delegated and lied, the expert who left out something, the initiate who didn't know, the preacher with the scarred knees.

The benighted, who want more stuff.

Who, not being able to tell, spat out the essence with the excess.

Ah, happenstance, that made of contingency a condition.

Ah, the twinkling of an instant, that made a likelihood of chance.

Big boys all, come blow your horns.

The cat's ascended who could tell us why opposites are one.

The homeless man who left behind a note: "Even if I had money, I would not buy *Anubis,* it frightens me so."

Who, asleep on the street, wrote: "I have been visited in dreams by a fox, and once by an animal like a large weasel."

2. More About the Dead Man and the Elusive

You will not rid yourself of the dead man at the margins.
You will not evade him or replace him at the edges.
Try to write it between the lines, his method is your madness.
Paint it outside the borders, his character is your fault.
Are you one of those students who does the assignment but misses
    the lesson?
The dead man drifts by in the aura of lost opportunity, pointing to a
    better misstep.
Yes, it is all true—what he said, what he meant, what he only suggested,
    what he didn't let on about.
While he was about, you might have asked, but you did not.
Your well-groomed erudition made the sucking sound of a bog as it
    confirmed you and likewise drew you in.
Did you think approval was a sudden intake of air?
The dead man hears the relief sought by gasping, panting, whispers
    and wheezes.
His time is the space between two hands about to clap.

The Book of the Dead Man (#50)

1. About the Dead Man and One or More Conundrums

Within range of the sodden fanfare.

A little fevered, to know in one's bones.

Undone, which is to say one awaits word in the province of eros.

The dead man has completed his task, he has hewn one capacious Gordian
      knot, he has shaved head-to-foot with Occam's razor, he has freely
      determined his immunity and renewed his license.

It is requisite to read between the lines, who are able.

It is best to deduce and intuit, who are skillful.

It is apt to stay the course if one would see the flayed reclothed.

2. More About the Dead Man and One or More Conundrums

Enthralled, the dead man lay waste to the picayune by gathering them
      into one.

To the dead man, the whole is partial and the partial whole.

One had only to watch the snow- or rainfall to see the truth exposed.

And what would the truth look like exposed?

Would it have sinew, would it have veins and arteries, would it throb with
      inner organs, would it cough and speckle and freckle and fret?

Would its dark hair turn white?

Would it labor, would it die?

The dead man is troubled by his close relationship to experience.

The dead man sees a conflict between experience and truth, as between the
      dark matter of space and the sticky stuff of the atom.

Particle upon particle the dead man heaps to slay the beast by its own weight.

The Book of the Dead Man (#51)

1. About the Dead Man and Taxidermy

Out of a suitcase of discards there came dead lilacs and a dead Abe Lincoln,
    and the dead man was there to see it.
From a posh trunk there spilled dead lilies and a dead Kennedy, and the
    dead man was there to see it.
From the heavens there rained explosives, and from the hills came the thud
    of mortars, and the Family of Man lay in pieces, and the dead man was
    there to see it.
The dead man studies taxidermy to better preserve the bailiwick.
He rearranges museums according to the ideals of moderation and
    proportion.
The dead man props a wax Plato by a cave on the road to town.
He puts a plaster-of-Paris bust of Aristotle by the gate.
He posts the heads of lions and elk on the top edge of the city wall.
He sends for the pickled brain of Einstein, the shreds of the dropped brain
    of Whitman.
He asks for a kidney stone taken from Pablo Neruda.
He runs ads seeking dried gall bladders, lung tissue, vocal boxes, eardrums
    and stringy veins.
He offers a reward for information leading to a heart.
He bribes the guard to better examine the pharaoh.
He rehearses the torture of slaves, POWs and prisoners of conscience to see
    where the parts fell, that he might retrieve them.
The dead man will put the world back together, wait and see.

2. More About the Dead Man and Taxidermy

It is as if you were a roustabout in outer space, collecting the burnt-out
    hardware.
It is as if you had been given the last stick and nail and sent to the beaches to
    draw forth wrappers and tops.
It is as if you had been given a carton of cigarettes to strip, the papers to be
    buried, the tobacco to be scattered.
It is as if you were just body heat, just temporal resolutions, just a mold
    without walls.
It is as if you had asked for it, as if you had missed a chance to decline.
It is as if you were for a moment the eyes of a packed moose head, one wing
    tip of a stuffed eagle, the whole jaw of a bear rug.
It is as if you were some fractured persistence, some ancient belief in thought.
It is as if you were suddenly laughable, mournful and senseless.
It is as if you were one of a kind by default, who killed the Buddha,
    contrived a less-than-ideal Plato, and mixed up Aristotle the sentry
    with your comings and goings.
It is as if you were gone today and here tomorrow.
It is as if you were the last one, out looking for a tar pit so that later they
    will know.

The Book of the Dead Man (#52)

1. About the Dead Man's Contrition

The dead man's acquired cackle is a kind of repentance.

His smile fills the gap between what was said and what he heard.

The shock wave of his metaphysics, pursuant to temporal civilities, carries
     within it his sorrowful greeting.

That ardor with goose bumps, that love of you that lay fallow, that passion
     for honey had to be cut short to survive.

Without penance, without reparation, without auras or whiteouts, neither
     active nor passive, the dead man's entreaties lift love from its matrix so
     that the lover can reach all the way around it.

The distance has narrowed between the known and the unmentionable.

2. More About the Dead Man's Contrition

It is as if the dead man employed a skull hammer to drive home his point.

It is as if he used a bone saw to separate the known from the unknown and a
     two-fingered wrench to grip the truth he once held in his teeth.

The dead man has slipped out of the lecture on flowers to explore a field.

He wends his way among specimen after specimen.

His apology may take the form of a basket of examples.

His explanation may seem an Etruscan code.

His exegesis may be no more than a pebble pitched into boiling lava.

What on earth! and How can he! and What next!

Folly to explain, what nonsense, what balderdash, what baloney.

Here lies the poetry of the twentieth century, consigned to a chauffeur who
     knew only the road to the cemetery.

The Book of the Dead Man (#53)

1. About the Dead Man and the Cardboard Box

Low sounds roll over the dead man in his cardboard box.

Infernal steam hisses at the dead man in his refrigerator carton.

The dead man had a cardboard fort, a cardboard playhouse, a cardboard
cutout, a paper doll, a boxful of shredded cardboard, now he makes a
nest of excelsior.

Is the dead man the natural antecedent to homelessness?

Who else knows the fact, suspects the truth, surmises the outcome?

Who else can make change?

The dead man seeks no other shelter than this, the elements.

The dead man accepts no other refuge than this, this asylum, this retreat,
this cloister.

Shall the dead man be buried alive—possibly.

Shall the dead man be left for dead—inevitably.

The dead man's cardboard box is a plaything next to the crates and cartons
of the homeless, the car hulks, the infested comforters, the littered
steam tunnels, the bins, the boards and the bags.

The dead man finds no trophy to the sublime in these ramshackle coffins.

The dead man refuses to go to his grave while people live like this.

He evacuates the heated halls of Congress for seats to sleep in.

He clears out office buildings, libraries, banks and post offices, and decrees
that decrepit vagrancy shall find its home in government.

The dead man stifles deconstruction of the homeless.

2. More About the Dead Man and the Cardboard Box

The dead man goes home, he goes back to where he came from, he goes to
      hell, he goes to some trouble, he goes to pieces.
The dead man sees the homeless go without.
He sees the paper cups of soup carried into the dark hovels of the down
      and out.
He sees the blankets and bedrolls in doorways and the newspaper insulation
      left to curl on the steam grates.
He senses the relief in all-night subways, twenty-four-hour waiting rooms,
      public restrooms.
He feels the sun restoring life after a cold night on the sidewalk.
He knows what it means to take medicine from a bottle.
The dead man hears the siren when they come to take a body from the street.
He goes to see but is shouldered aside by those who will take its place.
The dead man memorizes homeless math: one fewer means ten more
      tomorrow.
He sweeps up the broken vessels and used needles, the emptied sandwich
      wrappers, the paper and cardboard, the human waste.
He cleans up after those who have gone to make a living at the dumpster.
The dead man knows about salvage, scrap iron, scrap flesh.
The dead man is a homebody condemned to sleep in packing, fated to live
      among the derelict in the lap of luxury.
Shut in, locked out, germane or alien, the dead man enumerates the
      nomadic tribes of the cities—by box, blanket and bedbag.
The dead man finds out after the fact whether or not he has made the rent.

The Book of the Dead Man (#54)

1. About the Dead Man and the Corpse of Yugoslavia

When the dead man feels nausea, he thinks he is in the Balkans.

Feeling nausea, the dead man thinks he is scattered body parts.

Dismemberment makes the dead man queasy—historically.

Is not the dead man a witness to every dole, lot and quota?

Was not the dead man in place when the Serbs shelled Sarajevo?

The dead man heard the shouts of the victims being pasted into history over brief captions.

He pointed a finger at the butcher Milošević when the guns hammered the old city.

He shook his clenched fist at the genocide visited upon the Muslims, as it was and would be upon the churches, synagogues and mosques of the secessionary and independent.

He twisted and thrashed to transmit an underground murmur of conscience.

He gyrated, he spun, he literally threw himself into the air, he did everything possible to gain their attention but dance.

At a distance, the dead man's screams made a beautiful music.

Now the dead man, having lain down in flash fire and fire storm, bewitches his contemporaries.

The dead man proffers the scent of something left undone, but there are so few words for how a thing smells.

The dead man is the last one of many.

2. More About the Dead Man and the Corpse of Yugoslavia

The dead man sees the head, then the heart, of a dismembered State.

He sees the arms that tried to clap, the eyes that blinked and went blank and
were turned under.

He raises a fluttering flag held by the leg bone of the violated.

He hangs the dry tongues of the multitudes along the fences of western
Europe.

He mails the ears and lips to the West for overnight delivery.

The dead man is the inscriber of names and dates, the conveyor of last wishes
and words, secretary to a truce signed over the scent of cremation.

When there is no more defense, no strategic withdrawal, no bargain, no
outcome, no resolution, then of course there's no condemnation, no
horror, no moral reality, nothing intangible to impute dishonor to
the victors.

The dead man is the spoils to which the victors pledge their allegiance.

The dead man wonders why the hurry?

Meanwhile, the dead man certifies each eye extracted for an eye, each tooth
for a tooth: the whole carnivorous escapade.

The dead man picks among the living for future specimens.

The Book of the Dead Man (#55)

1. About the Dead Man and Famine

When the dead man feels pangs, he thinks he is in the Sudan or Somalia
    when the crops failed.
Feeling hunger pangs, the dead man thinks he is all bones.
Hollow cheeks give way to no-cheeks, a flat abdomen fills with air.
Witness the dead man fall in, line up, relinquish and shrink.
Was not the dead man taller once, heftier, closer to heaven?
The dead man passes his hands through the shadows of sagging flesh.
He points a skeletal forefinger at the water carrier and the cook.
He quivers from cold, trembles when the trucks thunder in with rations.
He pulls himself up by a gossamer thread connected to tomorrow.
He stands in the food line like a construct of bones half hidden by a
    dropcloth.
The dead man's stomach no longer rumbles.
Dried-up potions, bags of totemic remains, cosmetic invocations to
    universal powers, letters to the authorities now weight the air—
    immobile, debilitating artifacts.
The dead man sniffs the air with the last of his lung power.
His chips, shreds and tatters will be the good luck charms of leftover
    believers.
The dead man neither believes nor doubts but is nourished by half-measures.
The dead man is free to go.

2. More About the Dead Man and Famine

The dead man's condemnation would be for all time, so he does not condemn.
The look in the dead man's eyes widens to encompass four food groups, five
    grains, seeds and sauces, livestock and prey.
His famine is not a fast.
He rouses himself for a meal, he transforms his geometric figure—triangles,
    trapezoids—into the number "1," he jingles and jangles as if he were
    a dancer festooned with jewelry, but it is only the click-clacking of
    loosened tongue and groove.
This is not purgation but the good intentions of the fearful.
Who but the dead man can convey salutes, cheers and accolades to the
    starving in Somalia, the Sudan, those living in the eroding landfill
    from which the good stuff has been taken?
Who better than the dead man to welcome the Malthusians?
When there is no horrifying number, no catastrophe that cannot be
    miniaturized, no news too big for a box, no lack more immediate than
    others, then the dead man does not linger.
The dead man wonders not why but who.
He files the forms that will be found afterward, he fills in the blanks that will
    furnish the data, he obliges by coming to a full stop.
The dead man wonders not what but when.

The Book of the Dead Man (#56)

1. About the Dead Man and the Jury

Hast thou witnessed what the dead man hath witnessed, seeing the killer go
blameless and free?

Is it only that the dead man sees him slither, slide and sneak, dodge and
deceive, fake and feint, equivocate and prevaricate, and is that anything?

Is it simply, or satisfactory, that the dead man's weary of witnessing, and is
that anything?

The dead man witnesses the coronation of the coroner—sovereign of
fact's residue—sanding the rust from the knife, polishing the bones,
distilling the flesh, boiling the bravado, taking the measure of man, but
is that anything?

There sits the jury, replete, fraught, brimming, abundant, and the dead man
wonders, What is conscience?

Before them appears the judge, obvious, absolute, his robes of conviction
billowing as he walks in a murmuring breeze, and the dead man
wonders at the wherewithal that endowed every creature but mankind
with resolution.

The dead man banks the fees and delays, the sidebars, the recesses, the
motions and objections, the appeals and sentences, the fines, the
imprisonments, the executions, and with one strike of his gavel turns
them all into dust.

Is it anything at all, the dead man asks, to bear the sword and scales, to wear
the blindfold, to ask and answer, to overrule and sustain, to swear, to
promise, to pledge, to bargain, to settle?

Is there any for or against?

The dead man takes neither hostage nor loot, yet he has emptied the
vaults of their value, and he causeth the pricey counsel to cower with
self-knowledge.

When there is nothing but the client's good suit, the jury's self-doubt, the
    time since the crime, the charts and photos, the measurements and
    samples, then what knowledge is on trial, what rote redundancy passes
    for fact, what past lingers?
Where there is no more overriding impulse, no search for the truth that
    is not a battle to the death, no word left to meaning, no uncontested
    jurisdiction, no unacceptable flimflam, how then is a spinoff, a
    byproduct, an effect less significant than its cause?
The dead man did not yell "Fire!" in a crowded theatre.
He did not utter the word "containment" during times of genocide.
He did not use the conditional tense to describe the human condition,
    nor does he undermine the paralytic, the catatonic, but awaits an
    underground reckoning.
The dead man and his fellow dead are the jury whose verdict will out.
It is not the dead man's doing when a sentence contains the seeds of
    revolution.
The dead man was the first to arm the sentence.

2. More About the Dead Man and the Jury

When nothing more can be done, when the jurors have sunk into the
  sublime humus, the soft undergarment, the liquid center, the tender
  moment, the pliant interpretation, then guilt is merely innocence with
  an attitude.
The dead man deposes and subpoenas, he files the writ and registers the
  habitual corpses.
He witnesses the jurors bailing out, the bailiff glassy-eyed, the court
  reporter's finger stiffening from repeated movements.
He has heard family members flood the air with their tears.
He has seen the seesaw of acquittal and conviction pivoting between yes
  and no.
The dead man knows that the truth may be found inside the brick that was
  used as a club, on the handle of the knife that punctured and slit, and
  in the handprint on the gun that projected death, and he waits at the
  edge of metallurgy and ballistics for a degree of certainty.
The dead man burns the torts and briefs mistranslated from the past.
He stirs into the ashes of legal reasoning the unreasonable doubt of
  far-fetched scenarios.
Whether the case be deliberate or accidental, he leaves nothing to chance.
All shall be whitewashed, the stain lifted, the jury discharged without so
  much as a by-your-leave from the dumbstruck.
The killer was someone else, the victims are still alive, the weapon never
  existed, the alibi was too good, whatever it takes, paranoia, conspiracy,
  wrongful punctuation, the jury must be bled of its life force.
The dead man stores in time the hair, the blood, the fingerprints and
  mug shots, the withdrawn shoelaces, the shackles and cuffs, the
  trophies and souvenirs, the soap and tar, the sectioned buffet tray, the
  precedents, the testimony and visitations, and he wraps the severed
  finger in a handkerchief to call into question whether or not this finger
  was part of a hand at the time of the crime.

The Book of the Dead Man (#57)

1. "He is not Kafka and yet he is Kafka."

Like the hero of *The Trial,* the dead man is and is not.

The dead man is and is not mortal or immortal, is and is not menial or
maximal, he has and hasn't, he says and doesn't.

By his old clothes and worn masks he seems familiar.

The dead man hid himself in view, he led the sublime down the garden path
of public consumption, he captivated the masses with an empty bucket
and a hoe.

Who better than the dead man to dress up like a gardener?

How can the masters and mistresses of the moment break free to join the
roses, let the dead man do it.

The dead man serves the moment, he savors the crystalline instant, he
relishes and reveres each subdivision of time.

Naturally, the dead man enjoys the privilege of transubstantiation in sight of
an open door.

Inevitably and irrevocably, the dead man mates with all creatures familiar
and unfamiliar, who crawl, fly, swim or walk, those who stand accused,
those devoid of words, those abundant in rubble and salvage.

The dead man's caterer may someday serve tea in teacups too fragile not to
be beauty itself.

The dead man's agent may someday make of light and dark, and nothing
else, a garden beyond the grasp of prolonged sighs.

2. More About the Dead Man and Kafka

Nothing more than a white apron now holds a residue of the dead man's
   blood.
Condemned to be bathed, condemned to bleed, condemned to be
   sanctified.
The dead man offers his throat to the mirror.
He lops the curled ends from his beard, the squared ends from his
   fingernails, the bent wax from his ears and the roses from spring.
His is the union of the accused of another age.
His moment is dusk, his season is autumn, his time is late.
The dead man's independence counsels us to have done likewise.
His overarching abundance, worldly and other-, advises us from beyond.
The dead man knocks on the door as he would strike the chopping stone
   beneath his head.
He stands by the snorting carriage horses sprayed by their saliva as he
   would stand at court bathed in darkness.
The dead man is and is not an insect and a dog.

The Book of the Dead Man (#58)

1. About the Dead Man Outside

They came to the door because he was small or went to some church or
      other or was seen in the company of girls or boys.
Well, he was small and went to synagogue and didn't know what to make of it.
They said he was from some tribe, but he didn't understand it.
They acted as if they knew what they were doing.
They were the executioners of brown eyes and brown hair, and he happened
      to have both.
Well, he said, and they went away before he awoke.
They were a dream he was having before he became the dead man.
Today the dead man lives where others died.
He passes the crematoriums without breathing.
He enters the pit graves and emerges ashen or lime-laced.
He shreds the beautiful tapestries of history and hangs in their place the
      rough shirts and dank pants forsaken at the showers, and the tiny
      work caps.
He mounts the hewn chips of shoesoles, the twisted spectacles, the tortured
      belts and suspenders, the stained handkerchiefs.
Here, he says, is history, maternity, inheritance.

2. More About the Dead Man Outside

Let none pardon the Devil lest he have to begin again.

Let no one weep easily, let no one build portfolios of disaster snapshots or
      record the lingo of the know-betters, let no one speak who has not
      considered the fatalities of geography.

The dead man does not suffer skinheads lightly, their evil is legion.

With an olive branch, he whips the villains into a frenzy of repentance.

The dead man tattoos the war criminals with the numbers.

The dead man wonders what America would be like if every war were a wall
      engraved with the names of the lost.

Well, they said, he was from some tribe or other, and he didn't understand it.

When the dead man was a dead child, he thought as a child.

Now the dead man lives that others may die, and dies that others may live.

Let the victims gather, the dead man stays on the outside looking in.

Let the saved celebrate, the dead man stands distant, remote.

The dead man listens for the sound of Fascist boots.

They will be going again to his grave to try to cut down his family tree.

This time the dead man will see them in Hell.

The Book of the Dead Man (#59)

1. About the Dead Man and Consciousness

If numb, the dead man may think himself unfeeling.

If insensate, he may think himself indifferent.

He too rides the rim trail of alternative knowledge.

He too seeks prudence and insight, and would not become an old bottle for
    new wine.

The dead man believes that he must empty himself.

Time is moving through him, unwavering, insensate.

2. More About the Dead Man and Consciousness

In the domestic alphabet, the symbol for the dead man is a clothespin.

Like a duck's foot, the dead man contains four wishes.

He might have been a pair of duck feet, scuffling in the interminable mud,
    but instead he became a man of two minds.

He might have stayed in the center of the widening gyre, but he became
    instead the new atom.

The dead man did not set out to become a crummy dummy, any more than
    an infant sets out to become a man or woman of means.

The dead man is a means to an end, the later that defines the now.

The Book of the Dead Man (#60)

1. About the Dead Man and Less

Now the dead man quivers with increasing abnormality.
Increasingly abnormal, the dead man is a leaking battery whose next spark
    will be the last of its life.
Those who know, know.
What was in the beam of a flashlight that the dead man shone it at the stars?
Whom did the dead man signal, and who replied?
The dead man reads the semaphore of comet tails and meteor showers.
He wanders the night sky tracing the route of Orion.
He moves a flashlight among the constellations like calipers measuring the
    expanding universe.
The dead man giveth life unto the night.
None but the dead man can so render the illusion of eternity.
Here lies the dead man, not anyotherwhere.
Nor anywhere other than here shall the dead man be seen to have vanished.
The dead man waves the Milky Way before him like a magician's
    handkerchief.
He grabs the moon by its ears and lowers it into his outsized top hat.
He enraptures the planets by repeatedly bowing, drawing them closer even
    as they lean over the precipice of their oval tracks.
Why did the dead man smile to think the universe egg-shaped?
The dead man tosses his flashlight from hand to hand like the emcee at the
    last night of the year.
The dead man's light is incandescent and fluorescent, it flows through and
    around him, it spots and vanquishes, it follows a subject from first act
    to last, from stage to offstage, from balcony to footlight.
The dead man is awash in negative space, invisible in light but manifest on
    the other side of the merely dark.
He walks behind the plow as it shaves the sky of light.
The dead man does not come from this direction or that one.

2. More About the Dead Man and Less

To the dead man, all is written but not in so many words.

The dead man's voyage through space takes him to the edge of time, the
      border of breath and the end of anything more.

Hence, the dead man is less than his story, a good yarn.

The dead man fesses up, he tells and implies, he hints and reveals.

The dead man's diary is replete with bite marks where he sunk his teeth into
      the day.

When the dead man is thought about less, he becomes less to be thought
      about.

And where the dead man took less, he takes less yet.

For the dead man is a mote and a mite, less particular than an electron,
      subordinate in position to a neutron, groundless as a light wave
      content to arc above earthly illumination.

What does it mean, that the dead man is less but is no less than everything?

How can the world credit the dead man with all-or-nothing?

The dead man wagers less and less on each roll of the planet.

He wraps it up, he cashes in, but before that he so mixes up odd and even,
      heads and tails, high hands and bluffs, that the game goes under.

The dead man is a proponent of winner-take-less.

The Book of the Dead Man (#61)

1. About the Dead Man and the Late Conjunctions of Fall

The dead man heard a clucking in the trees at maple-sugaring time.

Today he feels a fibrillation in the curling leaves of autumn.

The near-frost lengthens his line of sight, bringing down the moon, while
among the spheroid melodies of harvesting, fate detaches the prospects.

The dead man fosters the free flying of the leaves.

He encourages deciduous trees to be done with dying.

There where the Anglo-Saxon and the Latinate meet anew, the dead man
bespeaks the continental drift.

There where body and soul conjoin, the dead man rejoins the indivisible
nation.

Who but the dead man can fashion a broom from a branch and discern the
seasons from wisps of sugar and pollen?

The dead man sandpapers flakes and splinters from the chair where the one
oblivious to time sits reading beneath burnt foliage.

He calls to the wild turkey in its infancy to stay still in the brush.

The dead man cedes supremacy neither to the body nor the soul, neither
does he stay in one place like a day on the calendar.

The dead man feels like the tree that was tapped for syrup, all in good time.

2. More About the Dead Man and the Late Conjunctions of Fall

The dead man readies himself for the ice skaters whirling overhead, their
blades crying *wish* and *wish*.
Which will crack in the brittle days to come, the dead man's ring or the dead
man's ring finger?
The dead man does not hasten, nor does he pitch his tent.
The dead man, like others, shall be departing and returning, for such is the
grandiloquence of memory in the junctures of separation.
The dead man attaches an epistle to a leaf, he discloses his whereabouts to the
harvest moon, he cranks forth leaflet upon leaflet to satisfy the scene.
The dead man's dying leaves, burning, appear as a crimson wash in the
autumn dusk.
His is the midnight light of high proceedings beyond the horizon.
The dead man will not twitch lest he frighten the little twigs from their
exposed roosts.
When there is no holding on, no letting go, no firm grip, no restoration, no
hither and yon, no arboreal refuge, then okay—say that the dead man
in his vigor watches it all.
He holds his tongue lest he sound the alarm.
He hears the fallen extremities swept away by the wind and remembers.
The dead man has written an elegy for autumn and a postscript to the
Apocalypse.

The Book of the Dead Man (#62)

1. About the Dead Man Apart

When the dead man opens himself up, he is blown about, showered, shed,
    scattered, dismantled, diluted and diffused, not discarded.
When the dead man is unfolded—unbent and unbowed—he is gathered,
    consolidated and collected, not condensed.
The melee, the chaos, the disorder, the tumult—the dead man sleeps.
Libraries drift past laden with coffins of illusion.
Things truly dead lie buried in the commercial tide, sweep in on the sea.
The dead man is joyful in the future of his having said so.
What to do and where to be in the millennium is of the moment.
The dead man's old eyes peruse and otherwise overtake the intentions of
    blood on parchment, divinations and forecasts, the jubilee of a century
    of anticipation.
The dead man signs on and off, his silence is his assent.
His irretrievable warrant must live in the henceforth and the consequences.
His ardor shall endure, though it sag with the dew point.
The dead man too had fits of loneliness, from which he has recovered.
He sank to the depth of doubt and fell past time into vast confusion, from
    which he has recovered.
He slept with illusion and woke with unreality, from which he has
    recovered.
He made the mistake of youth, the error of age, the blunders, the bloopers,
    the false steps of left and right and of the deceptively wide middle way.
All the dead man wanted and wants, he has.
Where the sun has forgotten the moon, where the stars have forsaken the
    abyss and the very footing has moved on, the dead man knows his place.
The dead man is forever flagrant.

2. More About the Dead Man Apart

The dead man knows that death does not shine in the dark, as the wind is
	not blown about.
It is up to the dead man to subject himself to the subjective.
It is the dead man's fate to be passionately detached.
Who, facing the end, better hikes, hurries, treks and tours?
Who but the dead man, having all the time in the world, dispatches his
	intentions?
Go thou, says the dead man, thou book born in ignorance, go thou and do
	likewise, otherwise, elsewise, be not timid among the blind specialists.
The dead man does not pluck, cull or garner reality.
When there is no end result, no picaresque interval, no immediate
	or impending, nothing imminent that is not also the past, then
	why not roses and rubles, peace and prosperity, and okay it's not
	inconsequential to have come and gone.
When the boat departed with the jackal-headed oarsman, the dead man was
	here and gone.
Then the horrific was infused with beauty, and the dead man lit a lamp.
The dead man's ashen look is the dun result of his volatile condition.
The dead man loves you because your habits slay him, you tap your foot to
	the music, and your heart blows up when you gasp.

The Book of the Dead Man (#63)

1. About the Dead Man and Anyway

The dead man has up-the-stairs walking disorder.

He has one-foot-in-front-of-the-other indisposition and other aspects of
      the wistful.

He has over-the-hillitis, the past-one's-prime predicament of week-old
      celery or last year's universal theory.

The dead man has a pox, a condition, an affliction, the usual entropic
      timing, the sudden parsimony of a reformed spendthrift, all of it born
      of the purest, simplest love: gratitude for having been.

What if the dead man's love were less, would that make your pear wrinkle?

What if the dead man's truth were unsaid, would that cause you to kiss
      yourself down there?

Come on, come off it, be upstanding, it's not all fruits and vegetables,
      peaches and cream, rubber chickens or joy buzzers.

The dead man never said he wouldn't die.

Anyway, the dead man is too alive to have been dead all this time.

The dead man is the light that was turned on to study the dark.

Where there is no more nonetheless, no before or after, no henceforth
      or regardless, then the dead man in his infirmity, deformity, and
      prolonged ability overlaps his beloved in riotous whatchamacallit.

The dead man's language for love is largely blue-collar whatchamacallit.

2. More About the Dead Man and Anyway

The dead man rubs salt in his wound anyway.
When the dead man finds in himself a hollow, he fills it with salt anyway.
A little torture is breathtaking for as long as the dead man can hold his breath.
The discomfort that will not let the dead man sit still is transformed into
      curiosity by late-night abandon.
The beauty of the horrific is bled of its human cost by the long night
      of shaking.
The dead man, after long silence, sings his way through the graveyards.
If there is any way to change pigskin to silk, the dead man will find it.
Anyway, he has only one or two lives to give for his country.
He has only himself and his other self.
The dead man will not be countenanced or counterfeited, he will not be
      understood by the merely reasonable, he will not bleed his wounds of
      their hideous glamour and come up pristine.
Those who would slightly reorganize the bones will find their vanity
      unrewarded.
Those who would take the dead man's head away will lose themselves in the
      topography of his skull.
The dead man stands for what things are, not what you call them.
The dead man stands for living anyway.

The Book of the Dead Man (#64)

1. About the Dead Man's Deathstyle

The dead man practices a healthy deathstyle.

Oh, who now can forestall the dead man's imminent passing?

What with every little thing, the dead man sits atop a system too gone in the
gut to go on.

Now is the dead man's time to be ransacked.

Hard materialism reveals the elastic character of reincarnation: either the
universe is finite, so nothing is ever lost, or the universe is infinite, so
nothing is ever lost.

It appears to the dead man that not to be is still to be, yonder and hence.

Excuse me, whispers the dead man, elbowing past like a penitent in
Zen vaudeville.

Forgive me, whispers the dead man, rehearsing an apology for your
imminent long memory.

2. More About the Dead Man's Deathstyle

The dead man will last, but not for the usual reasons.

In the circumspect annals of the dead man, no dead weight, no interlude
    that does not assert its count, no residue that does not rise to embody,
    no line on the oscilloscope that does not jump for joy.

The dead man has been *there,* and he's been *here,* and he likes it *here.*

Thawed blood flows back into numbed limbs.

A jumpy pulse increasingly interrupts the horizontal.

The brain's whirligig, each organ collects or refuses according to its purpose,
    each sensory aperture widens to receive the stimuli put on hold.

The dead man is shapely to surrender, trim to relinquish, tidy for the final
    presentation.

Let the grass flagellate the earth, still the dead man lingers.

Let the wind tug the hair shirt of the burial site, the dead man tarries.

Let the sky bend to see what gives, still the dead man does not give ground
    all at once.

The dead man cannot be done with, for his register and chronicle, his yarns
    and recitals, his rosters of lives shall be obsessively and incautiously
    annotated.

It is the dead man's way, for his penchant and proclivity have made of the
    green reed a whistle on which to solo.

The Book of the Dead Man (#65)

1. About the Dead Man and Sense

The dead man struggles not to become crabby, chronic or hypothetical.

He searches philosophy in vain for a pair of boots, a butterfly, a bent nail, an
      overlooked umbrella, some paste or scalp oil, but these new professors
      are all talk.

To the dead man, their theories are a kind of fretting, a way of blaming, a
      rightness carried to wrongheadedness, they have each other.

The dead man steps repeatedly into the stream, he does not wait for the
      water to be recycled.

His inclination is all downhill.

That's why the dead man likes all weather.

At bank's edge, he sees punk weed, tadpoles, pebbles that speak with mouths
      full of water, mud fit to be balm.

The water is less than it was to a fetus, but more than it will be.

How can the dead man explain water to these oversubscribed, arid
      phlegmatics?

A little water in the palm is worth the windpipes of a thousand tutors.

Helen Keller among these by-the-book tutors might still be waiting for
      a word.

Whitman's learned astronomer still prattles on about the distant stars, which
      for the dead man are at arm's reach.

The dead man laughs to see cold water thrown on language by those who
      are nourished by praise.

Their too many words have made a soupy alphabet.

2. More About the Dead Man and Sense

It would be wrong of the dead man to blame earth, water, fire or air.
It would be foolish to hold others hostage for a ransom that never existed.
It would be inescapably topsy-turvy to hold up to censure the material or
     the immaterial, the psychical or spiritual, the mental or emotional.
How curious now are the dead man's postures, struck in the dark for worms.
What on earth did the dead man imagine his frothiest words to be worth?
When there is no safe passage, no carriage wings, no golden ladder, no river
     to cross, no sage, no idiot, no ratchet-wheel big enough or lever long
     enough then okay the dead man no longer strives to move the earth.
He would be one with missteps and failures, of a piece with error and fault,
     united with blemish and blunder.
He would be, and he is.
The dead man's thought is visceral and unconditional, love as it was
     intended when the river met the shore.

The Book of the Dead Man (#66)

1. About the Dead Man and Everpresence

That one was lost at sea and another to rot, that one threw himself from
      a roof and another from a bridge, and that he, of these and others,
      deferred and delayed has been a long astonishment to the dead man.
That he should be the green soul is a shock and a stupefaction.
To what end was it begotten that he be known among his late friends?
Why hath he not perished as studiously as prophecy foretold?
He has pals, but not so many now, who, borderlines, go their own ways.
When there is no more sacred or heretical, no promise, no guarantee, no
      warrant that places the millennium, no voltage too high or current too
      strong, then naturally there can be no one side, no one alone, no other
      and no otherwise.
Loam or grime, clay or dust, the dead man penetrates and permeates, he
      pervades and saturates and otherwise occupies every veneer, wrapper
      and façade.
Likewise, he hath gone dry in the leaves to better touch them.

2. More About the Dead Man and Everpresence

Shall the dead man doubt the ax or the envelope, the tar or the hinge, the
    birthday candle or the rubbery moon?
It is longer and longer that things are as they are.
Shall he ask the river to be a capsule, the shoesole to be a clockface, the
    library paste to be rivets?
The dead man knows that the owl's hoot is also a searchlight, that an enamel
    doorhandle may become a beacon, that milk is also bone meal.
To be at all, the Whitmaniacal wonder of it, the Homeric—harsh register
    this age has come to, with all its data.
To be unknowing, through martial times or Chaucerian—soul-searing these
    days have been upon us.
The dead man leaves among the burned shirts, the shredded insulation, the
    free gases and syrups, amidst the upturned and rooted-out, hints of a
    trail made of basic materials.
Do not let them tell you that the dead man has gone on ahead.

The Book of the Dead Man (#67)

1. About the Dead Man's Further Happiness

If truth begins in heresy, then the dead man's capacity is the root cause.
If the future is famished, if every angel is terrible, then the dead man's
    appetite is to blame.
Tuber or bulb, grit or grub—the dead man is not above a bit the amalgamate
    malarkey of the underworld.
To the dead man, the abyss is not the pit it was said to be, but is elsewise
    and otherwise.
The dead man's refusal to mourn is notorious, gladly has he traveled in
    stateless realms: child of a universal Diaspora.
The dead man's shoes are too muddy, too shabby, to have been left to chance.
Do not assume, what with his high jinks and horseplay, that the dead man
    has not sometimes had the smile wiped from his face (Mister).
He, too, has been made to wish he was someone or somewhere else.
He, too, has been told to suffer in silence.
Yet he has flourished under the gun, been free in his chains, ducked and
    sidestepped his captors without moving.
To the dead man in solitary, alone with his thoughts, the world was two
    things at once.
Why is he, root cause and effect, happy and was he?
And why was he happy—and is he?
The dead man confounds the carriers of salt water who hang about looking
    for open wounds.
He misleads the bullies, the roughriders, the toughs and the thugs, he
    defuses, he disengages, he acquits, discharges and absolves.
The dead man's behavior befits the nearly departed, the temporarily
    indisposed, the tailored byproduct of our declination—here and gone
    in a jiffy, in a twinkling, in a flash.
Ah bliss, that fairly glories in the grave and the ephemeral.
Ah sensible gladness, that reflects equally the divisible and the divine.

For it is the dead man who recalls the sea to the shoreline where sandpipers print the beach.

And it is the dead man who summons from the ocean floor the clay to make the stone egg that safeguards the fossil.

For the dead man's rogue ruminations get under his skin, he worries and pleases himself equally—parent and child.

Yet his unhappiness was turned round as if it had met a wall and could go no further.

The dead man in his earthly joy has taken transcendence down a peg.

2. More About the Dead Man's Further Happiness

That he wanted to be there and not there was to him to feel desire doubly.

That he wished twice as hard was to him to manifest a method to his madness.

The dead man must be doubly peaceful to know peace.

He must be twice as ecstatic to fathom himself orgasmic.

He must be two times the man he was, twin to a twin, a voice congruent with its echo—twice cursed, twice blessed.

The dead man sees the armored crab take to the bait.

He smiles to see the bait take the crab and the tide turn tail.

He hears the slatted sides of his craft complaining to the waves.

He laughs to hear the salt water wearing away its knuckles.

The dead man risks the peril of your affection for a laugh that is also a yawp and a howl, and the hail that is also farewell.

Where there is no second sight, no reconsideration, no disconnection of wishes granted from dreams deferred, then okay good sense is sensory and grief a wispy exhalation of melancholia.

He who became the dead man was made to feel doubly: active and detached, refreshed and depleted.

The dead man's ups-and-downs are to him private peaks and valleys measured by their distance from the moon.

The Book of the Dead Man (#68)

1. Accounts of the Dead Man

The dead man likes it when the soup simmers and the kettle hisses.

He wants to live as much as possible at the ends of his fingertips.

To make sense, to make nonsense, to make total sense, lasting sense,
    ephemeral sense, giddy sense, perfect sense, holy sense.

The dead man wants it, he requires it, he trusts it.

Therefore, the dead man takes up with words as if they had nowhere in mind.

The dead man's words are peacock feathers, bandages, all the everyday
    exotica ground under by utility.

The dead man's book foresees a flickering awareness, an ember at the end of
    the Void, a glitter, a glow beneath the ash.

The dead man's book is the radical document of time, nodding to calamity
    and distress, happy in harm's way.

To the dead man, the mere whistling of a pedestrian may signal an
    onslaught of intention.

The dead man calls his spillover a journal because it sounds helpless and
    private, while a diary suggests the writings of someone awaiting rescue.

The dead man doesn't keep a diary.

The dead man sweeps under the bed for scraps, pieces, chips, tips,
    fringework, lace, filings and the rivets that rattled and broke.

His is a flurry of nothing-more-to-give, the echo of a prolonged note struck
    at the edge of an inverted bowl.

Now he must scrub his brain before a jury of his peers.

2. More Accounts of the Dead Man

The dead man has caused a consternation, but he didn't mean to.
He was just clocking his pulse, tracking his heart, feeling his way.
He was just dispersing the anomalous and otherwise scouting
     the self-evident and inalienable.
It was just that sometimes he couldn't stand it because he was happy.
It was the effect that he effected that affected him.
Some say it was his fervor for goose bumps took his breath away.
Some say it was the dead man's antsiness that put him in the dirt.
Some say he was too much the live wire, the living will, the holy spirit, the
     damn fool.
His was a great inhalation, wanton, a sudden swivel in the midst of struggle,
     a death dance with demons and other dagnabbits.
The dead man was well into physical geezerhood when he came to a
     conclusion and declared his independence.
At once he was chockablock with memories, the progeny of design and of
     blooper, boner and glitch.
He had his whole life to live.
When there is no more beseeching or gratitude, no seats remaining on the
     metaphysical seesaw, no zero-sum activity, no acquisition that is not
     also a loss, no finitude, then of course the dead man smiles as he blows
     a kiss through the wispy curtain of closure.
Some say the dead man was miserable to be so happy.

The Book of the Dead Man (#69)

1. In Which the Dead Man Speaks for Himself

Conclusively, concussively, decidedly—the dead man went beyond to reach
the limitless.

Love, faith, that which does good or harm, that which is neutral, that which
is dispensable, the selfhood of the artist, the selfless sage—the dead
man admits to being but one of many.

That there is still ego in observation, that there is yet self in the mildest
awareness of another—he cannot go further except he go no further.

I shall be speaking of the dead man with shut eyes and a writhing brain
besides.

I shall have to lay my head on a pillow.

It was the Army way through the long trench until he held, facing the guns
under bullet-tracings in a night sky.

One of many.

The dead man went over the top and beyond the pale.

He evened things up, he squared the odds, he made sense of rubbish and folly.

He was rapt and aroused, he was himself, within and without.

He was my particular and my universal.

I leave it to the future to say why.

2. In Which the Dead Man Speaks Again for Himself

That there was an I who saw it all—
When they poisoned the well, I babbled at the brook.
That one lived at the expense of another.
Always the last hoard of food, the final barrel of sterile water, and one
    solution was as good as the next.
The dead man notes the brilliant holding action, the rigor, that is
    civilization.
The dead man sponges up its literature and art, he travels in Space and
    observes microcosmic innards without his presence distorting the
    works within.
But the dead man cannot do this to himself forever.
The cows are out there but they won't come home.
Hell's fires are banked but they will not freeze.
Was he not, forage and the Devil besides, the happiest dead man alive?
I thank him, whom I shall not see again in this life.
He makes me smile.

The Book of the Dead Man (#70)

1. About the Dead Man and the Picket Fence

Ten to one, the one in question made it home safely.

Everyone was glad the party was over, and the séance had ceased that was
    seeking the lost art of conversation.

The three metaphysicians left early.

The seven alchemists did not come out of the kitchen all evening.

No one brought up the red leaves of sunset, there was not a hangnail to be
    seen, nor were shoes mentioned, nor saw blades nor carburetors, nor a
    pencil with an eraser nor the shell of a crab nor the imaginary eyebrow
    of a hummingbird.

It was as if a world without turtles hastened time, and it took a universe free
    of glue, spittle and the secretions of bees to tour space.

A world without means or ends, a world of process without a project.

2. More About the Dead Man and the Picket Fence

Always to be the swirl blown into the bottom of the glass bowl, the finger
    marks on the stoneware, the ember that went upward as the kiln fire
    reached cone ten.
The dead man reconstitutes the story of the blind man who could see, the
    deaf man who could hear, the mute who could speak.
Nor scuttlebutt, nor buzz, nor yarn—reports of a dead man who lives have
    been documented.
The dead man was seen scraping gum from the sole of his shoe.
His wool cap and thick trousers were glimpsed going down an alley.
He was seen from a distance placing a white egg on a picket fence where no
    one would see it.
His presence was detected in a darkened movie house.
He was observed without his knowing making snowmen and mud pies,
    sand castles and leaf piles.
His fingerprints appeared in the clay.
He was seen trying not to be seen the day the sky fell.
Everyone loves the shine of the ordinary, the dead man too.
All may study the rainbow, the dead man also.
Not a man or woman does not envy the owl its privacy, the dead man besides.

from **Mars Being Red**

(2007)

The Book of the Dead Man (Ghosts)

1. About the Dead Man and Ghosts

The dead man travels land, sea and sky to look for ghosts.

The dead man has seen them in the clouds, in smoke and vapors, paling in
fog, rising in the surf, dancing in the flaring embers of campfires.

He has heard them shaking the bamboo, whistling in the wind and the
graveyard, flapping the roof shingles, drumming on the walls,
whipping the power lines until they sing.

He has smelled the soap and softener of clean sheets.

He has tasted the residue of incense that appealed to them.

He has felt the timbers shiver, the moonlight stutter and the air cringe.

There was dread approaching, and it might have been the ghost of history
coming to extract payment.

There was weather in the air and the tent flaps slapping.

There was a drumming at a distance, or was it steps on the stair?

The dead man's little pinky bone was still attached after the campfire had
been soaked and the scary tale was over.

The dead man will not recover his mortal friends though he welcome
their spirit.

The dead man has seen ghosts appear to those who wish to make peace
with death.

He has sketched the human figure in the northern lights, in constellations,
dust devils and waterspouts.

They appear in the distance.

2. More About the Dead Man and Ghosts

The dead man cheers for the Ghost Dance and all invocations of spirits.

The dead man has seen what his country did to its natives.

He knows that their spirits must rise up in the living.

He knows neither apparition nor daemon, neither the ethereal nor the
      incorporeal, neither the soul nor the specter shall turn back time.

Only the citizens have power who invoke the dead.

The dead man has counted the bodies of those who lived on ghostly in
      a cause.

He wants to believe the ghosts of Jefferson and Adams will overthrow
      the fascists.

For what good are ghosts who are pretty Pollys or skull bones, guilt-trippers,
      hand-slappers or buddies up from the egocentric psyche?

The dead man's ghosts have guts.

He hears them on the street corners speaking from the mouths of the rabid.

He sees them wrestling invisible opponents in doorways and alleys.

He waits for the day an army of ghosts lays waste to those who slaughtered
      the innocents.

The dead man will haunt America until it does right by its unseen.

Until then, or until the Earth meets the sun, he is not going anywhere.

The Book of the Dead Man (Memory)

1. About the Dead Man and Memory

If there had only been a window to the past.

If there had been a smear of belladonna, a hint of an alphabet in the smoke, a
flame licking at the extraneous, a drumroll to announce the meaning.

The dead man poked his memory as if it were coals.

When he raked the embers, they sweat sparks.

If there had been a glass through which one could see behind oneself.

If the scissors had not marched inexorably down the seam.

He'd have been happy to scrape by, casting yarns of land and sea into the
soapy foam that kept cleaning the shore.

If there had been a magic pill, a fire-walking epiphany, a panacea under the
photographer's cloth.

Never mind, the dead man has made his getaway.

Like an umbrella wrenched by the wind, like an egg rolling downhill, like a
wagon without brakes, like sirens that won't stop, the dead man is here
and gone.

Where on the globe, where in the cradle of civilization, where in the garden
of figs and exotic mosses, will he find the past?

The dead man rings up the millions who tried.

He gathers the bones and artifacts in baskets, he piles the buttons and
buckles, the knives and numbers, the shoes and boots.

In a twist of fate, under a lilac sky, kin to mica and calcium, the dead man
rests for a moment, considering.

He knows the latest, but he is not telling.

2. More About the Dead Man and Memory

By now there are dead man poems all over the earth.

Dead man and dead woman poems.

If there had never been Dadaism, Surrealism, Existentialism, the Absurd or
    the Prophetic, there would never have been a dead man poem.

If there had never been unreality.

If there had been no mind, no knowing that one knows.

If there had not been etymology, if the insects had not multiplied.

If there had been only the affections and affectations of the sublime, as the
    sun slid from arc to arc.

If there had never been a post–World War, there would have been no
    second dead man poem.

Now nostalgia regrets its big shoes and calloused footprints.

Now the backyards of nature are the gardens of a former world.

For it was dead man nature to separate, to carve out, to homestead and stake.

It was Dead Man and Dead Woman who came first.

If the water could not breathe, if the steam grew heavy with grit, if the cloud
    burst with particulates, if dew encrusted the grass, if eating an apple
    became the mask of resistance, the dead man could still pull up the
    blanket.

If there had been a floor that did not give way, a philosophy that could sew a
    red thread through stone, an underfoot that was glass.

For the dead man looks up and down as he kisses the yellowing clusters of
    lilies that signal a breaking fever.

The Book of the Dead Man (Recent Dreams)

1. About the Dead Man's Recent Dreams

Call them ravaged castles in the air.

Think them fancy, fantasy, reverie or romance.

Dismiss them as head trips and chimeras.

He sees them day and night, call him a woolgatherer or stargazer.

He cannot stop his seeing what is not there.

Call it the prior future or the posthumous present.

For his sight when asleep is that of a brain loosed from the mind.

The dead man shuffled the deck, he crumpled the map, he trashed the
     tea leaves.

Now he must strain to hear the springy squeaking of life among the
     deciduous messages of fall.

Think him the fool, if you like, who speaks in riddles.

He has become the willful naïf, the one who closed his eyes to better see.

For now there is only the sea sweeping.

There are only the clues left gasping when the tide recedes.

2. More About the Dead Man's Recent Dreams

The dead man's dreams disappear in the light.

They make no promises, they are the body's dance, they are happenstance.

Who has ever died in his dreams and told?

He cannot see the face of the one whose hand reaches for the door.

And have not many of his visions taken the bit and run from view?

He has tried repeatedly to go to sleep in his dreams.

The dead man is not one to go flying while asleep, he is grounded.

He has walked hot coals, lingered among auras, and been taught if one says
      a thing three times it will happen.

Wake up, he has said to himself, wake up, wake up.

He has blamed his dreams on the hour, on life, on a bite of sweets.

He knows that dreams are not an effect but a cause.

Last night he spoke aloud the word "joker" but does not know why.

He dreams of living forever for a few minutes at a time.

The Book of the Dead Man (Time)

1. About the Dead Man and Time

When the dead man rises from bed, time smiles.

Time itself snickers at the dead man rising from bed.

The chortling sounds in bells and buzzers, radio whispers, sunshine fizzing
    in the leaves, the wheat and corn rustling from near and far, the ten
    thousand things to be remembered.

The clock face laughs at his ache to be active, as the moon laughs at his
    lethargy, his ennui, his apathy, his teetering between means and ends.

The dead man is the liquid that stained the antique veneer.

He is private.

He has a hammer in his ear, a pin in his knee, and a knot in his groin.

He is a rake passé and a married man.

The dead man offers time . . . more time.

He hath washed the lamb and the linen and ironed the work shirt.

The dead man, dead and alive, is an instrument of war and of peace.

Neither cotton in his ears nor a turn of the knob can stop the mental
    pictures he makes from the evening news.

In the control room, a stopwatch measures the bones to be unearthed, the
    depth at which a soldier sticks in sand, the several times the field cook
    turns the ladle to serve the troops hot meals.

The dead man thinks time is not the measure of time.

Bodies are a measure of time, the smell of loess is a measure of time, the
    taste of roots, the feel of the shrunken and putrid, a whistle fading as
    the mourners walk from the gravesite, the moon circling is a measure
    of time.

The dead man and his counterpart are a pair.

They have looked up from the lowland and down from the bluff, they
    have slept on a rug and a bench, they have slumbered in a box in the
    framework of time.

The dead man has time on his side and time in his pocket.

He has had a taste of time, and he likes it as much as cake or a pear.

The dead man lives equally in Newtonian time and Einsteinian time.

As the world hurries to convert uranium, the dead man feels for time's edge.

2. More About the Dead Man and Time

The dead man did not plan to teeter between life and death, here and there,
      or now and then, it just happened.
It was not his doing when the cotton shirt wrinkled for good and the
      instruments could no longer be tuned, it was time.
It was time that turned the big ladle in the sky.
It was time that wore out the rug to show who had come and gone, it was
      time loosened the bed frame so love creaked.
The dead man does not believe in time but sticks to the subject.
He does not believe in time but in the time it takes.
For in time the sun will fizzle, and the bone, potsherd and tooth unearthed
      by the archaeologist's rake are the records of time.
Who knows time better than the dead man?
The dead man knows that time is the other face of no-time, the backside of
      an alarm clock, the knob turned to Off that controlled the fatal gas.
Time that stopped for Houdini is more than magic for the dead man.
Time is the unseen liquid that oils the edge of the earth.
Time is the invisible pin that fixes the moon above.
Oh, time in a box, time on the head of the nail before the hammer strikes,
      time that takes the silkworm by surprise, time that bluffs at night, time
      that washes the wheat.
Time that releases the sound of the cowbells, time of the time clock at the
      end of the workday.
The dead man does not applaud time, but what men tell of it.
Under the veneer of time, life and death pair up to iron out their differences.
The dead man knows he alone cannot stop the stopwatch.

The Book of the Dead Man (Writing the Dead Man Poem)

1. Writing the Dead Man Poem

When the dead man writes a poem, he immediately writes another one.

He writes another because two follows one.

So well does part two shadow part one that they cannot help but argue
    and marry.

He who would write a dead man poem must know that all things coalesce.

She who writes a dead woman poem must understand that perception is
    kaleidoscopic.

The dead man sees and hears every tangent, every approach, every blade of
    grass that bows this way then that.

When the dead man repeats himself, he never steps into the same line twice.

The dead man, after midnight, turns the key that coils his insides.

His poem lasts as long as his innermost spring remains compacted.

When the dead man's spring snaps outward and bites, then the poem has
    ended that defined the moment.

A dead man poem knows that the sentence is the key.

The sentence, sans enjambments, has redefined free verse.

Yet it is not the sentencing on the page alone but the sentence of time.

The dead man serves the sentence, he fluctuates between the long and
    short of it, between the finite and the infinite, between the millisecond
    and eternity.

Whosoever shall write a dead man poem must know in his bones that his
    lifetime is an event that splits another event in two.

That is why a dead man poem must have two parts.

You may think at any moment you are done with life—so many first
    thoughts, so many smarts, such agility—but you are not.

Later, you may think you had only begun at the finish, so complete was your
    escape from time while writing the dead man poem.

You may be discordant or discombobulated or delighted to feel the weight
    of a dead man poem.

For a dead man poem threads and disentangles, sews and slices, glues and
    fractures.
Its harmonies are made of missing notes and from words he would gladly
    take back.
It is in the dead man's mission to show up the illusions of time, the discrete,
    chaos, order, health, and whosoever misuses quantum mechanics one
    day and the death of armies the next.
Write a dead man poem if you must, but only if you must.
For the dead man hath no choice, he hath only blind luck and love.
He hath only his prophetic existentialism, his diary of the posthumous.
The true dead man book can be opened anywhere to the fullness of life,
    what else was poetry ever for?

2. More About Writing the Dead Man Poem

It is also necessary to understand the abandonment of distinctions.

To realize that a poem can be forbidding yet ephemeral, while a dead man
      poem may run from side to side or seesaw yet carry the gravity of
      the ancient.

Why this is so is of a matter embedded in mortality.

So deeply buried that vanity cannot mine it, it will take poetry
      masquerading as prose, philosophy hiding in the impulsive, the devil-
      take-the-hindsight, shotgun-riding, seat-of-the-pants voice of the very
      now without regard for itself to express the consolations of time, and
      to say for once the solace Jacob felt wrestling the angel.

Do I surprise you with my reference, very well then, I surprise you.

I invite you now to write the dead man poem, the dead woman poem, the
      poem of the dead chorus fluttering the weeds with song.

For only then will you be one among the many, your intentions subsumed
      in something larger than the self.

Your sentences must be elastic, your thoughts flexible, your heart given to
      the hidden acrobatics of dark emotions.

That is all I can tell you.

To help you any more than this would be like the rain instructing a cloud—
      too late, too late.

The dead man is plugged in, he is the last vestiges of dead friends, he suffers
      the little children to grow up and away.

He hath lasted the lashing of night, he hath wrestled the angel to a draw.

Few will know how lasting his love.

For you cannot write a dead man poem if you have not known love.

Vertigo: The Living Dead Man Poems

(2011)

Live as if you were already dead.
(Zen admonition)

The Book of the Dead Man (The Alleys)

1. About the Dead Man and the Alleys

The dead man, bowling, hit the head pin.

Thinking he was dead-on, he was, it was the sign of the times, the human
condition, his wanting the wrong thing.

With the one pin knocked out, the dead man was once again in a life of
dichotomy.

Now he looks at the 7-10 split and wonders, which side?

He can't help seeing the split as life and death, chance and no chance, public
courage and inner cowardice.

In the classroom, the tenth frame would be final, the eleventh a probation,
and the twelfth an afterlife.

Here, if the dead man tries to bounce the seven off the wall and across the
alley, it will take dumb luck, it could happen.

The pin boys have their legs up, why not try.

If the dead man tries instead to slice the far edge of the ten and skitter it
across, it will be once-in-a-lifetime or the gutter.

Here, too, is the human condition he remembers, writ in hand dryers, rental
shoes, tenpins, duckpins, candlepins.

The raucous, shiny leagues filling the lanes, the monorail of balls thudding
up into line.

And the chart of boxes, for the one inclined toward fractions and addition.

The beer frames, the whiskey frames, the turning away after a roll and
looking over one's shoulder to see if of course . . .

2. More About the Dead Man and the Alleys

Now the ball hooks sharply, and the pins dance.
The asymmetrical core is something like our new selves.
The dead man has known the stone balls of kegel, the pre-modern
      ironwood, the hard rubber before resin, urethane, and particle balls.
He has seen the weight the world put upon the shoulders of these new
      bowlers, even as the weapons grew lighter.
He can sense the new ball picking up oil as it rolls.
He can see the ball hook sharply into the pocket as if it knows.
The dead man's human and inhuman conditions have melded.
Someone else may not know what it was to be the pin boy hurrying to
      dodge the impatient early roller and earn tips.
There are perfect games galore now, is it still bowling?
The dead man knows that a new tool, like a new cadence, is a new idea.
He didn't have to be an Imagist to see what's up.
He didn't have to be a Cubist or a Futurist to see what was coming.
It still sounds like a wingding, it still feels like a jamboree, it's the heavy ball
      headed for you-know-what.

The Book of the Dead Man (Anubis)

1. About the Dead Man and Anubis

The dead man, considering, was asked, "When is the right time?"
What if one were whisked away too quickly to be missed, not even the smell
     after a lightning strike, not even the mist of a teakettle just turned off.
Ah, but the dead man is more resilient than the grass, more recollected than
     the jalopy of first romance, more encrypted than the crypt.
He outlasts the red dross of old blood.
He outlasts the clockwork, he lengthens the leap years.
The dead man may lie safely under a palm tree, or cross the barbed wire.
He cannot be harmed by a coconut, he is not a target on the battlefield.
Now he is beyond both the local and the larger, out of range, calmly of a
     piece with gravity and the genuflecting universe.
Let him furrow his brow, it doesn't matter.
Let him wrinkle like the pelt of a cheetah or bloodhound, either way.
He survives any comparison.
All time is the right time for the dead man, but in time you may miss him.

2. More About the Dead Man and Anubis

The dead man will find you.
He has befriended the weigher of souls and keeper of tombs.
He is the I-Thou of what matters for a while, then less.
Hence, the dead man repeats his pleasures in memory.
He loves the swish of the broom, the crease in the bedsheet.
He hears as well the music of the rattletrap as that of the wind.
He feels the weight of *more*, the heapings of the world.
He calls the pot black, he lounges till noon in his reading garb.
The dead man outlasts the low sky, the soggy, the arid, the freezing,
    the sweltering.
He has vaulted the horizon, he has dispersed the material.
Here come the worms, is it time?
Turn here to see the dead man riding in the rumble seat.

The Book of the Dead Man (The Arch)

1. About the Dead Man and the Arch

In the curvature of space, in the ox yoke of industry, half-encircled by the
   arm of the rainbow or earthly in the curled palm of an open hand, the
   dead man lives ahead and behind.
The dead man's back arches as he bends to see or leans back in submission.
The dead man has ridden within the hollow arch.
He has scratched at the stone arch, feeling for the Etruscans.
He thinks the arch may follow the path of their lost language.
The dead man sees in the arch an incomplete zero, a footless oval, a hoof-
   guard, French arches triumphant, arches written in Utah by erosion.
Arthritic fingers are arches, and the flood-curled covers of art books, and
   the torso of a kneeling prisoner.
In such manner is dead man's geometry displaced from purity of thought,
   even as the age echoes with the latest "Eureka!"
Oh, purity of intention, beauties of foresight, and the fork in the road.
For it was the divergent that sent one uphill or down.
It was the creation of options that sent the brain reeling, the economy
   spiraling, and invented mixed feelings.
Then came the arch of architecture, which limned entry and exit, the yes
   and no, the business of going in or staying out.
Every arch is academic, for the arch that props a bridge or roofs a tunnel is a
   theoretical proof.

2. More About the Dead Man and the Arch

Ogee or reverse ogee, three-centered or segmental, triangular, equilateral,
      parabolic, the shouldered, the elliptical.
(About lakes, Auden wrote, "Just reeling off their names is ever so comfy.")
And his favorite, the "rampant round."
So doth the arch aspire from the ground up.
What better can this life be described than as "rampant round."
The dead man has stood on the arches of his feet, minding his fate.
He has fallen in with ideas with dirt on their shoes, arch-like.
He has worn out the merely sensational, that does not arc.
The dead man is not arch, but loves the arch as a geezer at the end of the
      Greek alphabet lifts a tumbler of ouzo.
Yes, the arch trembles at the chance to be both the beginning and the end.
The dead man, like you, entered through an archway of effects.
Everything is water if he looks hard, it is all a line over the horizon, a circle
      spreading outward from its core, a tilted parallelogram leaning on a
      wormhole, it can be the floor he falls through.
It is what he passed through and under.

The Book of the Dead Man (Arroyo)

1. About the Dead Man and the Arroyo

The dead man blesses the new arroyo.

The dead man knows that the arroyo is a gulf and a gulch, a gap and a gorge.

He has seen words fall into the abyss.

He has clamored on the way down and gasped on the way up, gripping the
    sides of makeshift handholds.

He has himself carelessly tossed what he meant to say over the rim.

He has both feared the edge and regretted his distance.

For it was in the topographic scheme of the art to propose to a muse in the
    dark, and who knew?

The long picaresque adventure of trying to say a life took place on a rim trail.

Turning back in sight of the waterfall . . . there came the two wolves where
    there were not thought to be wolves.

They were dead ahead, coming, and the dead man sought a stick but in vain.

Was the dead man making this up, was he the lie that tells the truth?

Then the dead man saw the wolves split up and go down and reemerge high
    on each side, watching.

Now when the rain comes and rises in the arroyo, the dead man wades
    in memory.

He of the wolves in the wild, he of the well bucket, he of the ragged creeks,
    he of the waters within him is of a piece with all that washes away.

Pour your heart into the dry arroyo to be nourished and run off.

Empty your mind into the parched crevasse to be filled and dispersed.

All of it will have its moment.

You can bring it up.

2. More About the Dead Man and the Arroyo

The dead man supposes he sees the sun rise from a promontory at the canyon.
He is able to do this because he did it.
To remember, for the dead man, is to do it all again.
The dead man can dance as if for the first time because he hears again a
     new song.
He can read new words in the shape of old ones, there is a crackling on the
     paper as they are born.
Were it not a planet with a molten core, the dead man could not stir things
     up so.
The dead man has blurred the edge so that now the arroyo is the dead man's
     mountain ridge.
The indentations in the walls of the arroyo are the dead man's foothills.
So that all that was thought to be descending, now ascends, and here
     he comes.
You cannot step on his speech, but the dead man's lingo will get in your head.
When there is no more paper, no ashes, no balsa wings, no feather blanket,
     no cloud cover, no omen, then upstream and downstream are the same
     stream.
When the rains come, when the squatter pebbles are evicted, when the flood
     is born and the wash is awash.
The dead man has been reading from underneath.
He has peered up through the four elements.
He has peeked between the flames and into the cracks.
He has peeled the dew and held his breath.
What better for the dead man than an arroyo, a chasm, hollows and ravines?
The dead man stands down to see up.

The Book of the Dead Man (Big Eyes)

1. About the Dead Man and Big Eyes

Would it have been news if space aliens had landed?

Late-night radio said it was old news, embedded in Stonehenge, crop circles,
    sky lights, the Pyramids.

The dead man was up late listening to the reports of space travelers.

Think of the dead man as a big head with huge eyes.

And the dead man's fingers carving disembodied scribblings.

The dead man cannot span an octave, and he types with two fingers, he has
    to look.

Like a camera, he squints to lengthen the depth of his field and bring the
    future into focus.

The dead man's eyes have seen too little or too much, it depends.

When the dead man opened the blinds and looked out, he saw farther into
    himself.

It widened his eyes, it dropped his jaw, it made his hands flutter to flee.

2. More About the Dead Man and Big Eyes

If the prisms of the eyes were not the prisoners of the brain.

If the eyes were not the windows of the soul.

If the soul were not incarcerated in the notion of a definite shape.

With every quantum measurement, the dead man is expelled from another
    universe.

Hence, he is multiversal, inside and out.

If you don't want to talk about it, the dead man understands.

When the Dog Star shines in his eye, the dead man blinks.

A time exposure to record it would take centuries, and he blinks.

If the soul was an eye, if the window was a door, if the brain was as plastic
    as space.

The planet will not be leaving without the dead man.

The Book of the Dead Man (Boomerang)

1. About the Dead Man and the Boomerang

The dead man stands still, waiting for the boomerang to—you know.
He hears the words of philosophers ricochet among chasms and disappear
     in the far away.
His scent goes forth, his old skin, hair and nails, and he spits, too.
He leans forward to look backward, and the ancient world reappears.
It is the beginning, when mountains, canyons and seas were new, before the
     moon had eyes, before paper, before belief.
Any words he utters now are souvenirs of the future.
They will be meant to keep a pestilence from returning.
They will be meant to string together a path to follow in the dark.
The dead man will ask who you are fighting for, do you know, will it come
     back to haunt you?
He will ask about the taste of ashes, he will ask if you remember.

2. More About the Dead Man and the Boomerang

The dead man's army swept the battlefield and brought the war home.

It was a time of troop surges and redactions, leaks and fire starters, a time of
bush-league government.

The dead man's zest for words went local, it came home to gravel underfoot
and mud under the eaves.

The dead man knows that all invasions are boomerangs, ask Napoleon, it
rains on every parade.

The dead man fingers those who will be revisiting the wars they began.

He high-steps to pass over the casualties who left their thirst on the sand
and their bones in the caves.

The dead man, too, is waist deep in gore, his belly full, his balance sheet
bleak, but no deadbeat, he will be heard from.

The boomerang effect has been building from war to war, campaign to
campaign, unit to unit.

A clicking of dog tags.

An army of medics and morticians.

The Book of the Dead Man (Borders)

1. About the Dead Man and Borders

The dead man is an immigrant, an exile, a local and a foreigner.

He came across the dry border or the ocean.

He walked, he rode, he sailed, he flew, he traveled miles on his knees.

He may have come by way of shadows, moving only in darkness.

He may have traveled without shoes, with little food or water, but still he
    carried his story, his temperature, his elemental rhythms.

Now the dead man feels a chill as the barricades rise.

He has the past in view, its clues, its nuances and hints, perfumed by a wisp
    of safety.

The dead man has proffered his passport for close inspection.

When the dead man rode a bus from Slovenia to Italy, the guards dragged
    his luggage from the bay.

And when he took the train to return, a sea-legged policeman yanked his
    suitcase from the overhead.

It was he whom the man in the dark coat followed around the dissident art
    show come to Venice from Russia.

What is it about the dead man that made him a target before the antiwar
    events had even begun?

The dead man can still feel the fist that missed, passing close by where he
    stopped to eat in the tavern.

He has known the armies to conscript fathers and mothers.

He has seen them composting war's fodder.

He has seen the massed volunteers whose forerunners had to run to his
    country for their lives.

If there was enough time between a wink and a nod, perhaps someone
    would replace the Welcome sign that was torn down.

If there were dollars to go around, if there were health galore and
    ambiguous tea leaves, then the dancing might last longer.

If it had not been necessary to crawl or duckwalk or roll over.

The dead man does not know where to place the line between here and
there, them and us, like and dislike.

The dead man hath married the haves and have-nots till death do they part.

The dead man lives on the life-and-death border, above which he hovers,
looking to this side and that.

The dead man is a realist.

2. More About the Dead Man and Borders

The dead man does not take sides.

He has crossed the big river, he has joined in, he has worn the lone Star of
David and the ankh, the good luck rubber band, the medical alert.

He has carried his address in his pocket, just in case.

The dead man knows that every homeland dies and is reincarnated and tries
to recover its past.

Look at his struggles to be more like this one or that one.

The dead man, too, was born into his bias.

The dead man, like you, has been skinned alive by the historians who
needed parchment to write the story of the victors.

The dead man knows the drill.

He knows where to stand to be let go.

He knows how to blend in, he waves the übernationalist flag on the holiday,
he scans the frontier.

There must be something about the dead man that raises suspicion.

The dead man's skin is of many colors, perhaps that's a red flag.

The dead man speaks the languages some take for code.

The dead man limps a bit, which reminds them.

The memory of an injury makes them crazy to see the dead man limping or
grimacing or just breathing hard.

The dead man does not want to see the aftermath of the explosion, to stir
the ashes after the fire, or pull the victims from the rubble over and
over throughout his nights, but he does.

The dead man is free to be fatally sensitive, he has been left to his feelings,
his blubbering, his inner aches, his embedded limitations.

The dead man is a realist with reasons, does that help, can he stay?

Will the dead man cross over with last words?

The dead man has friends all over the world who will hide him.

The dead man has invisibility on his side, so where is he?

The Book of the Dead Man (The Boulevard)

1. About the Dead Man on the Boulevard

The dead man was out walking on the boulevard when he looked up.

There, over his head, was the famous silver lining.

The street was as wide as the wingspans of four turkey vultures, he could
 look up and up.

He understood that the silver lining was related to the lateness of the hour.

He had eaten the chocolate kisses, he had used up the leftovers, he had
 ordered takeaway.

When he walks, the dead man reaches beyond his arms, he strides beyond
 his step, he unscrews the vise of three dimensions.

Here is the silver lining of tomorrow's sun at storm's edge.

(Did you guess that the dead man is out walking in a thin rain?

In the gray drops falling that blush when they hit the pavement?)

The dead man can do this in his sleep, in cloud cities, in stories he populates
 with people who also walk.

2. More About the Dead Man on the Boulevard

For the dead man, the world enlarges as he walks.

He is unable to look straight ahead, he catalogues the window dressers, he
      sets the mannequins in motion.

(Did I mention the light rain clearly enough for you to see it?)

Go walk the boulevard when the young couples are circling and the mothers
      watch their unmarried offspring like hawks.

When the late light alchemizes the air, when the sun falls into the net.

Each sensory selection uses up the dead man until he moves on.

It happens in a jiffy, in a flash, in a tick, in what youth calls a sec, it is all and
      everything for as long as anything.

If it were not for the lateness of the hour, everything he sees would be
      too much.

At the café, he dispenses the advice of one who has hiked the past.

The dead man's thoughts lengthen his years, straighten his bowed legs, and
      oil his lumbering, stumbling, strolling and skipping walkabouts.

The Book of the Dead Man (The Box)

1. About the Dead Man and the Box

When the dead man wants to deaden his brain, he surfs the channels.

He rides the Bonsai Pipeline of twenty-four-hour cable news.

He hears the field reporter, covering a death, pun on a grave experience.

He sees the reporter push a microphone into the face of the widow.

And the basketball sideliners asking players about giving 110%.

The dead man is 50% half-involved.

He thinks TV news is one long Jay Letterman, David Leno show.

He thinks the public forums have been Oprah-sized.

The pancake, the wigs, the stagy confessions . . .

He sees the ads for bad drugs and rollover cars and the disclaimers that flit
     past under low fares.

He hears the claims of the Ponzi brokerages, the gold hawkers and the latest
     minting of memorial coins.

His ears are filled with the incessant hawking of the latest murder, mayhem
     and marketing.

He switches among the evening reports of the three major networks: the
     stylish, the sentimental and the earnest.

The dead man has seen the Johnny-come-latelies come and go and the good
     one-in-a-million.

He remembers ugly Joe Pyne's wooden leg, quirky Ernie Kovacs' cigar,
     cackly Steverino Allen's fedora.

Now he labors to tell a thousand young actors apart.

He hears humor where there was none.

2. More About the Dead Man and the Box

The dead man lives in the flickering tube-light of rampant capitalism.
But if he wades through the smog of ads, there may be a late-night movie.
*Casablanca, Bagdad Cafe, My Favorite Year, The Stunt Man, Lawrence of
     Arabia, Slap Shot, Matinee, Duets, Without a Clue, Brassed Off, Men
     with Brooms, Funny Bones . . .*
Like lives, they end, each in turn, while warfare is serialized.
The dead man finds interstices in the American experience where people
     live who would never sell their story.
The dead man knows that there was never any news, just information.
He watches the news for the latest candidate, the big mudslide, the endless
     weather, the car chases, the Amber Alerts, the evangelical, the pogroms
     and genocides, and the latest worldly laundry.
The bad tidings encase his heart so that no single hurt can break through
     the tidal analgesic of the daily news.
He struggles toward late night hoping for no more news.
Music, dancing, humor and repartee squeeze through the airwaves.
The dead man believes radio blooms inside his head, while TV dies on the
     skin of his eyeballs.
The dead man thinks the telly should light up at midnight.

The Book of the Dead Man (Camouflage)

1. About the Dead Man and Camouflage

When the dead man wears his camouflage suit, he hides in plain sight.

The dead man, in plain sight, disrupts the scene but cannot be seen.

His chocolate-chip-cookie shirt mimics the leaves in a breeze.

His frog-skin dress, his bumpy earth nature leave us lost and alone, his
mottled apparel sends us in circles.

His displacements distract and disabuse us, he is a slick beguiler.

Everything the dead man does is a slight disruption of normality.

He is the optical trickster, the optimum space-saver, the one to watch for.

He is of a stripe that flusters convention, he is the one to watch out for.

That we thought him gone only proves his wily knowledge.

The dead man has lain unseen among the relics of embalmed time.

He was always here, always there, right in front of us, timely.

For it was not in the dead man's future to be preserved.

It was his fate to blend in, to appear in the form of, to become . . .

Now he lives unseen among the lilies, the pines, the sweet corn.

It was the dead man's native desire to appear not to be.

2. More About the Dead Man and Camouflage

The dead man knows that camouflage is all in the mind.
He has seen in the human need for shape the undoing of shape.
He has witnessed the displacement of up-and-down, across and slantwise.
He has curled the straight lines and unbent the curves, he has split the
      wishbone and painted outside the lines.
The dead man has undone the map by which to get there.
It is not what the dead man looks like, but what he no longer resembles.
For he hath reappeared in no disguise but as himself.
Call him disheveled, call him disposed, call him shiftless, he is.
For he hath been made and remade in the form of his surroundings.
He hath become all things that he looketh like.
Hence, he has been stepped on by those who could not see him.
He has been knelt upon by those who looked in vain.
The dead man bestirs in a background that looked inert.
The dead man is the ultimate camouflage.
He is everywhere, but where is he?

The Book of the Dead Man (Collaboration)

1. About the Dead Man and Collaboration

When the dead man joins up, he monitors the monitors.

The dead man, enlisting, pictures the pictures.

He moves among the moving, wiggles among the squiggles, yes, he laughs.

The dead man is part of a new language in the offshoot, unpronounceable
yet tip-of-the-tongue.

There will be birthing and splicing, fusing and fluxing, a Gabe and a Jacob,
a Scott and a Larry, two Stevens, one Anmarie, and the dead man
detecting.

He sees the trees morph into pixels, the text glue itself to the air.

Now hyperspace fills the room.

Now the dead man lives on, embedded in the universal retina.

Will universal collaboration create God?

Only the dead man has pictured it, seen it, absorbed it.

The dead man takes in sight and sound, stillness and movement.

Like the quantum cat, he can be in two places at once, he can move and stay,
he alone can be what you wanted and did not want all in one.

There is no stopping the dead man, who is perpetual.

There is no cessation of the life force a-borning.

The dead man tunes in online and offline, from Earth and space.

Once launched, the sights and sounds, the signals and sense travel through
time, tidal waves without water.

2. More About the Collaborative Dead Man

The dead man is perforce an installation.
Buried or burned, hung up in the body lab, doled out to the organ banks, he
 is also rooted in memory.
In his disassembly he is assembled, in his dismantling he is established.
Now he is set among the trees and the leaves that paint the air.
Now his skeleton becomes the ridges and fissures of the planet.
His is the ultimate collaboration, the reciprocal to its nth, the true mutual.
He is a proponent of the big shebang theory.
The dead man is the past, present and future, an amalgam of atoms and
 strings and the who-knows-what of bespectacled theorists.
Meanwhile, he wiggles among the squiggles, he mops up the washes, he rolls
 on the scrolls, he whirls within the whorls, he goofs in the gyres, yes he
 laughs and laughs, and yes he squirms among the worms.
He is the ready affiliate.
He is awash in the senses.
He lives among those who have mixed eyefuls and earfuls, oil and water,
 who have alchemized the elements and written in the pitch.
This now is the roadway of the dead man, united in every state.
The dead man shuffles his senses, he flicks, he riffles, he ruffles and rumples,
 he puckers and crinkles, he wrinkles, he scrunches, he stretches, and
 oh yes he struts a little, too.
Behold the dead man at the still point of a turning.
See the dead man painting by infinite numbers.

The Book of the Dead Man (Conversation)

1. About the Dead Man's Conversations

The dead man hath spoken with Matthew Arnold about ignorant armies.

He hath cautioned Keats on the isolate love of beauty.

If there were ever Grecian odes on the shore, they were smashed in the
    general onslaught.

Like sand castles adrift in the idea of architecture, like bas-reliefs planed to
    the texture of papyrus, like rubber in acid, the repositories of beauty
    did not outlast the idea of them.

The dead man is of a mind, and a mind to, and his exploration has been in
    the places where an idea may fit.

It has been a long thrill in the dark for the dead man and friends.

The dead man is on the side of art but also on the side of artlessness.

Absent the blank page, the word must forever be muddied.

The words can be true only to one another, like Arnold's lovers—the ideal.

Well, says the dead man, what have we here?

It seems the dead man has caught the words in a compromising position.

This verbal interruptus is aquiver from circling an invisible vase where the
    lovers have been trying to catch one another.

Must poetry forever be anticipation and delayed gratification?

The dead man has been talking with T.S. Eliot about escaping one's
    personality, which he has.

And with Wallace Stevens about the mind in the act of finding what will
    suffice, which he has.

The dead man, too, can write the tautologies that cloak war and torture.

But he no longer cottons to the aesthetic tilt of a head, the legendary voice,
    the prophetic boom box or starlit ego.

Why should the dead man use up his life in the usual ways?

The dead man's poetry is not stone-cold soup.

2. More About the Dead Man's Conversations

It was cold in the coffeehouse where the dead man met the editor.
The dead man had asked Henry James if there could be two congruent
    points of view.
He had challenged William James to a bout of automatic writing.
The dead man won the game of exquisite corpse when he folded the
    paper twice.
He wrote faster and faster, but he could not get down everything.
The engineers were of a mind to map a brain—an empty brain.
When the dead man and the editor met, it was in the early years of the
    Apocalypse.
That no one could conceive of everything had given the lie to prophecy.
It was a time when string theory was unraveling, when relativity had
    become absolute, when Gurdjieff's "all and everything" subsumed the
    cults, clans, castes, tribes and schools.
The dead man's papers had been overwritten.
It was up to the editor to select a sample.
The dead man has lived among remnants, shards, fragments, doubles and
    replicas, among lucky error and deliberate effect.
Like a snake, the dead man molts, leaving a whole skin now passé.
How shall the editor edit the seamless if not with scissors?
The dead man has been talking to James Joyce about not being there when
    his words end up new.
The dead man has been talking to Galileo about the law of falling bodies,
    which applies.
How shall the editor edit the perpetual or eternal if not with scissors?
The dead man's world is kaleidoscopic, it turns without stopping.
Say you knew him, but not what he was thinking.

The Book of the Dead Man (The Crossing)

1. About the Dead Man and the Crossing

The dead man hath been assigned to the children.

They stand on one side or the other, fidgeting, waiting to cross.

There will be a signal, a light, a flashing, and a dead man or woman in the
    middle of the street.

It is time to cross, says the dead man.

There are things to do so that you can do other things, says the dead woman.

The dead man remembers being an immortal child.

He recalls the daze of schooldays, the waiting to cross.

He, too, hurried through the stopped traffic to scuffle at recess.

He, too, watched the silhouettes through the frosted window of the
    classroom door after hours.

He, like you, felt the emptiness of the corridors.

He would take the senior trip to the Capitol and whisper under the dome.

It was long ago, and he was crossing without a guard.

He was not yet seething with ragged theories.

He curried desire, he lacked iridescence, he sank from failure.

He just wanted to get to the other side, like they said to.

2. More About the Dead Man and the Crossing

Clap quick, the immortal child is fast becoming the dead man.

The dead man who is alive and also dead.

He crosses repeatedly whatever there is to be crossed.

He shows up in the street before classes begin, stopping the cars.

He hurries the students to classes, but after school they hurry themselves
    themselves.

He stands in the street like a deciduous tree as they run past.

When the leaf blowers restart, the dead man knows what to do.

He may have tinnitus from the car horns, he may this day be scarlet from
    the chill, he may be fatter than last year.

Still, he is at peace with the one fact that most informs science, puzzles
    philosophy, and troubles medicine: that things end.

The dead man stands in the street, not letting the children cross just because
    they think they want to.

They are children, their lives are waiting.

The dead man, as a crossing guard, does more than required.

He is amplitude personified, he is the future withheld.

He waves, he beckons yes and no, he stops trouble in its tracks.

To the children, he is just arms and a rubber coat.

The Book of the Dead Man (Cutthroat)

1. About the Dead Man and the Cutthroat

The dead man steps guardedly around the fallen, picture the battlefields.

The arms and legs are the pick-up sticks of war games.

Who were these unfortunates who couldn't move out of the way?

Were they the sons of senators, clad in legacy blazers?

Were they the daughters of governors, atop the cavalry of their
thoroughbreds?

Here is why they cap the radio mic in foam or a stocking, no popping, no
spitting.

They are cutthroat who stop for no one, some are politicos, some are
commandos, some are little more than retail.

The dead man remembers the mom-and-pops driven from Main Street by
loss leaders at the chains.

What are we to do in a world of absolutes the dead man rejected?

The dead man spat his experience at those with the knives, it was dangerous.

2. More About the Dead Man and the Cutthroat

The dead man would be of the primary cutthroat trout class, one of
freshwater and not inclined to migrate.

Let the salmon climb ladders, let the salmon die in the gasp of the life force.

Let schools of salmon exhale to blow down the trees as they perish.

We little ones, like the cutthroat trout, we the meek, we shall inherit.

We will sputter with the hook in our mouth but say nothing more than spit.

Fishermen of the deep do not want our language, they live for the ocean.

The open sea is a cemetery, the open sea is a past century, the open sea is
too big for us.

The river is where we live, the lake, the canal, wherever we can be at our
throats with kisses or with knives.

It is not so far to one another that we cannot get there.

It is not so far to one another that we may not get there.

The Book of the Dead Man (The Dare)

1. About the Dead Man and the Dare

The dead man edges toward the precipice because he dares.

He dares to wake the audience.

He is of a mind to taunt and defy, to provoke and to goad.

The dead man urges the stuntman to repeat his death-defying spectacular.

He dares the trapeze artist and the wire walker to flaunt their nonchalance.

He is of a mind to exploit the acrobatic.

Where in the lexicon of good government did threat and menace
    replace courage?

The dead man is a reminder to the lawmakers.

It was dead men who won the revolution.

It was dead men who wrote the laws.

It was dead men who armed the citizenry that they might turn on
    one another.

It was dead men who defended the cities, and it is dead men whose names
    are etched in the town squares.

The dead man dares to tell you what you know you know.

The dead man would have dared more, had he known the outcome
    of waiting.

To the dead man, existence is like a bungee on which he must fall and rise,
    and fall again, until the distance is erased between up and down.

It was a split-second decision to take the cord and jump.

The dead man was a thought that became tactile, became palpable, some
    like to call him corporeal.

The dead man is the overarching presence, the coverall that let him kneel,
    the tarp that covered the weapons, the canvas bag, the muslin sail, the
    percale sheet, the cotton handkerchief into which he breathed.

Tell him you know.

Cover your mouth if you need to, but speak up.

2. More About the Dead Man and the Dare

The dead man has been afflicted by life, no complaint there.

The dead man does not make more of it than it was.

How best to call out the unjust and violent, the barons, the conglomerates, the cabals, the cartels and all who rise on the bent backs of others.

It is the dead man's place to call them out.

Everyone believes a dead man, and all men are dead men, we can get together and dismiss those who are daring us to.

The dead man says you know.

The dead man lives serenely in the backyards, in the surrounding farmlands, by the sides of ski trails and firebreaks, he is the one who will be coming from every direction.

The dead man's studies do not conclude, his decisions are not countermanded, the outcome of his being both here and gone can only mean that there will be daring.

The dead man has endowed daring in the arts but also in the streets.

He has fomented peace and made himself present on the battlefields.

He has placed himself in the way, who will step over him?

Now he asks you to whistle up your daring.

The dead man thinks there is enough in the dumpsters to feed an army.

The dead man hears the senators in the cloak room.

To the dead man, their language is flame retardant, their speeches are the cracking under the ice.

The dead man will turn the page if you will.

The dead man will lie prone to see into the abyss if you are beside him.

The dead man does not dare to say how happy he was.

It was the daredevil moment, when he decided.

He dared, he chose, he spun round, and in time the ground settled.

Here he stands, the dead man in his composure, but do you dare?

The Book of the Dead Man (Decomposition)

1. About the Dead Man and Decomposition

The dead man has a mulberry bush on the brain.

A mulberry chopped down thirty years ago, not one others can see.

It grew by the house, it was immediate, it was personal.

The dead man is of more than one mind about it.

The dead man's nature, like his brain, has been etched, chiseled, planed and
    diverted by a single bush, tree or flower, by a moment as quick as the
    claw foot of a bird overhead.

It takes little to inscribe in the dead man the forefront of the mystery.

To the dead man, that one mulberry was more than a forest.

To the dead man, the heron in his cedar was more than a rookery.

The dead man evades the notion of species to count by ones.

He is himself a species unlike others.

Others may sense, perceiving the dead man, that the silences of nature are a
    welcoming, and the sounds of nature are cautionary.

The dead man's love of nature, like yours, must be cognizant of the end.

It was not nature invented time.

It was not the devotees of entropy who said to live and let live.

The nature of nature will not be replicated in poetry ink.

The dead man greets Aristotle in the mindscape of imitation, it is not
    re-creation but a new world.

Such is nature to the dead man that the world may be endlessly reborn.

Even as the long dead live on in the dead man, so a mulberry bush may
    stay behind.

2. More About the Dead Man and Decomposition

Have you been waiting for the dead man to compose or to decompose?

The dead man, in becoming, unwrites and unsays.

The dead man has left no tracks in the loess, not in the humus, the loam, the
      dust, the salt or the talc.

Not in the peat or chalk, the silt, the gravel or the spilled feed.

His footfalls in rain and snow lifted off, into the ethereal.

The dead man's weight is not dead weight but disperses, aerated and released.

Your memory of the dead man is a child's balloon, and where is that off to?

Of the dead man, still there remains the whole of nature.

In the whole of nature, the dead man is of many forms, a thread, a mesh, a
      graft, a skin, and the spine of the natural.

The dead man does not save for posterity, he dispenses with drafts, he
      lightens the future for his children.

He is out ahead of literature in this regard.

It was the *what* beyond words that made him speak to you this way.

Take a line from it when anxious, for it will compose you.

You may remember it, you may memorize it, you may take it to heart, it will
      endure in the interstices of time.

For here the excerpt is a whole, and the whole is an excerpt—it is so.

The Book of the Dead Man (Drugs)

1. About the Dead Man and Drugs

The dead man tried to read the small type, but it was too small.

He tried to listen fast when the pitchman covered the side effects.

There was little to do but risk it.

It was the new drug for everything, a panacea.

He would no longer prowl the beaches looking for a word in a bottle.

He would not need to decipher the markings of crab shells, tea leaves, coffee grounds, the crystals or the clouds.

There would be no meaning of life, just life.

Then, in time, the dead man would feel a pain that had no name.

The side effects were death after one dose, muscle atrophy after two, kidney failure after three, there was a list.

The dead man has been on his knees, looking for a pill that rolled off the counter.

He has counted out dosages, placed the vials at bedside, woken himself in time, stayed up for the last, all that.

He knows that each pill is a concoction, like a cake, eat it all.

Each has its own way of defining a life.

So the dead man favors placebos.

As for body parts, he prefers to use the ones that hurt.

2. More About the Dead Man and Drugs

It hurts to stand up, so what?

It hurts uphill and downhill, as it should.

The dead man caught the general apathy toward the sociopolitical but
      dispelled it through better chemistry.

He thought hard, the way a high-jumper pictures his approach and his
      clearing of the bar before starting.

The dead man's foreshadowing can make something happen.

So he saw himself on a road away from the battlefield.

It is true, he could turn imagining into ability—the power to walk, say, first
      pictured, then realized.

The dead man is too corporeal for hallucinogens.

His drug is late nights, his obsession is now and its aftermath.

The dead man's drugs are not remedies but food for the overtimes.

They would be cure-alls, magical, miraculous, were they not dated.

The doc's charts show when time will run out, but it's a guess.

When the dead man is told he cannot walk, he walks.

He laughs at pain, he has a lot to learn.

The dead man is a geezer, and he is happy to hurt.

The Book of the Dead Man (Faith)

1. About the Dead Man and Faith

The pathway drooped on which the dead man walked.

It snaked, it undulated, it thinned out like molten glass on the blower's pipe.

In some circles, Vesuvius was thought a twist on the notion of fate, a wrinkle
    in the measurement of an Edenic Fall.

The dead man smiled and watched.

He read about the saints, thinking he could do good.

He studied rituals, thinking he might take this or that plunge.

He investigated the super-realistic and unreal paintings in Roman churches.

The pained Caravaggios, the hosts of madonnas and infants, the star-
    crossed disciples.

How many sought to escape the flesh.

The artists put gold in the sky, they pierced their subjects until they bled.

2. More About the Dead Man and Faith

The painters wrinkled robes and curtains in their art for effect.

They lashed the sea, they added thorns to the foliage.

They assembled crowds of believers clad in rags.

The dead man noted the rough grain of their faith.

He took stock of the commissions that fueled the glorifying.

In the dark chapels where a coin lit the art, there was also the dank history
    of laborers.

Thus the dead man inflicted disbelief on the framed narratives.

Outside, bits of pigeon soot bleached the walls.

There was a poster of a rock band, to appear in the near future.

Their faces mirrored and crowned the dead man's doubt.

The Book of the Dead Man (Food)

1. About the Dead Man and Food

The dead man likes chocolate, dark chocolate.

The dead man remembers custard as it was, spumoni as it was, shave ice as
  it was.

The dead man talks food with an active tongue, licks his fingers, takes
  seconds, but has moved on to salads.

It's the cheese, it's the crunch of the crunchy, it's the vinegar in the oil that
  makes a salad more than grass.

The dead man has a grassy disposition but no cow stomach for flappy leaves
  and diced croutons.

The dead man remembers oysterettes as they were.

He recalls good water and metal-free fish.

Headlights from the dock drew in blue claw crabs by the bucketful.

A flashlight showed them where the net lay.

If they looked bigger in the water than in the pail, they grew back on the stove.

It was like that, before salads.

The dead man, at the age he is, has redefined mealtime.

It being the quantum fact that the dead man does not believe in time, but
  in mealtime.

2. More About the Dead Man and Food

The dead man's happiness may seem unseemly.

By land or by sea, aloft or alit, happiness befalls us.

Were mankind less transfixed by its own importance, it would be harder to
     be happy.

Were the poets less obsessed with the illusion of the self, it would be more
     difficult to sing.

It would be crisscross, it would be askew, it would be zigzag, it would be
     awry, it would be cockeyed in any context of thought.

The dead man has felt the sensation of living.

He has felt the orgasmic, the restful, the ambiguous, the nearly-falling-over,
     the equilibrium, the lightning-in-the-bottle and the bottle in shards.

You cannot make the dead man write what you want.

The dead man offers quick approval but seeks none in return.

Chocolate is the more existential, it has the requisite absurdity, it loosens
     the gland.

The dead man must choose what he ingests, it cannot be anything goes in
     the world the world made.

So we come back to chocolate, which frees the dead man's tongue.

The dead man is every emotion at once, every heartbreak, every falling-
     down laugh riot, every fishhook that caught a finger.

The Book of the Dead Man (Foundry)

1. About the Dead Man and the Foundry

The dead man hath founded the dead man's foundry.
He acted in the past perfect, he funded it with clean dirt, pure water and the
    spotless air.
Then he was melted, he was molded, he was poured and shook out.
He was ground and sanded, he was machined to a sweet tolerance.
The dead man took pains to stay alive, this was how.
It was the undersong of the self, the subtext, the no-man's-land's calling.
For the dead man was subterranean to start.
He was the tuber in the sun, the worm warming, the root that stays put.
The dead man became again what he was, he germinated.
It was the foundry of the sun, the foundry of the earth's core, the foundry of
    the electric light and the dry cell.
It was the retrofit energy that did it, the assemblage after dispersion, the kick
    in the pants we call chaos.
We are the children of a hothouse, among orchids that grow in lava.

2. More About the Dead Man and the Foundry

The foundry of the dead man pops and smolders with re-creation.
It is re-created in the titanic and the miniature, every detail.
Within the dead man, the same fire burns.
The same furnace, the same raw materials that made flesh.
The same red water, the same liquid sinew cooling.
The dead man's foundry has made weapons and plowshares, and those who
     use them.
The foundry and the forge, the shapes imprisoned in the molten streams of
     rough matter, these are precursors of the human, too.
The steam escaping from a wounded body is the foundry.
The heat of exhalation, the blush of desire, the red sun under the skin—they
     are the foundry.
And the high temperature of the ill, and the heat of the first foundry
     reassembling at its source.
If you believe in the reformation of energy, then you believe as well in the
     dead man.
He is heating up, and what is emotion?

The Book of the Dead Man (Fungi)

1. About the Dead Man and Fungi

The dead man has changed his mind about moss and mold.
About mildew and yeast.
About rust and smut, about soot and ash.
Whereas once he turned from the sour and the decomposed, now he
    breathes deeply in the underbelly of the earth.
Of mushrooms, baker's yeast, fungi of wood decay, and the dogs preceding
    their masters to the burnt acre of morels.
And the little seasonals themselves, stuck on their wobbly pin stems.
For in the pan they float without crisping.
For they are not without a hint of the sublime, nor the curl of a hand.
These are the caps and hairdos, the mini-umbrellas, the zeppelins of a world
    in which human beings are heavy-footed mammoths.
Puffballs and saucers, recurrent, recumbent, they fill the encyclopedia.
Not wrought for the pressed eternity of flowers or butterflies.
Loners and armies alike appearing overnight at the point of return.
They live fast, they die young, they will be back.

2. More About the Dead Man and Fungi

Fruit of the fungi, a mushroom's birthing is an arrow from below.
It is because of Zeno's paradox that one cannot get there by half-measures.
It is the fault of having anything else to do.
The dead man prefers the mushroom of the gatherer to that of the farmer.
Gilled or ungilled, stemmed or stemless, woody or leathery, the mushroom
      is secretive, yes, by nature.
Each mushroom was a button, each a flowering, some glow in the dark.
Medicinal or toxic, each was lopped from the stump of eternity.
The dead man has seen them take the shapes of cups and saucers, of
      sponges, logs and bird nests.
The dead man probes the shadows, he fingers the crannies and undersides,
      he spots the mushroom underfoot just in time.
When the dead man saw a mushrooming cloud above Hiroshima, he knew.
He saw that death was beautiful from afar.
He saw that nature is equidistant from the nourishing and the poisonous,
      the good and the bad, the beginning and the end.
He knew the littlest mushroom, shivering on its first day, was a signal.

The Book of the Dead Man (His Hats)

1. About the Dead Man and His Hats

The dead man has the face for wearing hats.

He has the hair for hats, the ears and eyebrows, the wrinkly forehead, the
graying temples, a chameleon ability to fit in.

He has a way with the peaks of caps to be worn on rivers, on a prow
seesawing toward the sun.

Even when, at the end, the deserts are turning to salt.

Even without a shirt or shoes—he will have a hat.

He has a talent for finding a scorpion in his boot, or in a hat on a chair.

He has a talent for stringing together what others think ashes.

He has crawled the field in a helmet, he has stood in the corner in a dunce
cap, he was bar mitzvahed in a yarmulke.

He has danced round Astaire's top hat where it caps the Fred & Ginger
edifice in Prague, it was hollow, it was lofty.

He has walked Havana, Managua, Belgrade in contentious times, incognito,
private in a hat.

He has a method for shading his eyes, call it a knack.

He wears his cap backward to run with a kite by the sea.

His favorite is a feed hat, a crumpled plasterer's cap that touts what farm
animals eat.

2. More About the Dead Man and His Hats

Winters, in a watch cap, he sits at the café, a philosopher wrapped in an
     odor of strong coffee.
The dead man can wear any hat, that of Pan or Dionysus and also of that
     dour fellow, Chaos.
To the surrealist inside him, the moon is a mothball in a closet of fedoras.
To the realist in him, a covered head is how you get away when you find
     yourself on the target.
To the futurist in him, the dead man's hat is what's to come, he can just
     make it out if he pulls down the peak and squints.
To the cynic and soldier, naturally, every hat is a helmet.
His beret has a built-in tilt, and his hard hat a dent.
The dead man does not come to you hat in hand.
He has a hatful of thoughts he never mentions, nor does he spit on the plate
     when invited for dinner.
Like you, the dead man has kept a lot under his hat, and still will.
The dead man is neither a youngster nor a show-off.
He is the architect of an underground hat culture.
He wears a hat because he can't be taking the time to comb his hair.

The Book of the Dead Man (His Health)

1. About the Dead Man's Health

At least one exotic plant—an orchid, say.

At least one uncommon mineral—chromium, perhaps.

Bandages, tourniquets, splints, casts, wraps and salves.

The dead man continues patching where he can, covering the damage,
    propping the skeleton, reinforcing the shell, repairing, reinventing.

Here he is in the archway, hesitant in the corridor to the doctors.

There he is at the rooftop balustrade, his coat open, proclaiming
    unintelligibly while the white coats urge him down.

His health is but a distraction.

He finds himself again and again in the amphitheaters of the obstinate.

How to prove his sentences are philosophical gadgets, stand-ins for
    numerals from another plane, standards for animal behavior?

The dead man hears the selfish ones refusing to feel.

Their millions are increasing, whose skin cannot breathe.

The dead man carries water to the tar paper shacks.

He tells the poor the way to the nation's Capitol, they should know.

2. More About the Dead Man's Health

The dead man's *zero amount* is your *never ever.*
His treatments of the body politic require roses bearing thorns.
His remedies for innocence need water and wood.
The dead man and the dead woman have had words with our senators.
The dead man is not up to refusing you health care, he is different.
Have you heard about the dead man in pajamas, his months in bed?
He was given a long claw for picking up things, it was his toy.
His legs were as thickly wrapped as a panda's, comical, ungainly, diminished.
To be undiminished is the dead man's goal for health care.
Universal care belies a fixed number for those who raise its standard.
So the dead man's medicine is not a gel to make things shine.
It is gristle and bone, heart and soul, and spit for polish.
The dead man cups an ear to listen for the healing.

The Book of the Dead Man (His Olde Ode)

1. About the Dead Man's Olde Ode

The dead man has been writing the oldster's olde ode.

His oldest ode was the beautiful song, the sound of living at all.

Now ye olde ode is also the news.

Even if there were times when the horizon arced over the planet too acutely
    to reveal the others.

Even if the dead man could not turn enough to see them.

And if the keening of mourners was daily to be pulverized by the sound of
    motors departing.

Yet the engine of the planet purred, and the wheel sang.

So it was the nature of all and everything that absorbed the dead man.

The world was full of nameless things that words could not keep.

Some wanted the dead man to disown the silence, and he considered it.

He had heard how scary the silence could be.

He knew that an ode to joy had to be thumpingly hearable and make the
    floorboards bounce.

The dead man knew, also, that things end.

His hope was that he be free in the glare of truth to bask in the warm-up to
    the furnace.

And of course to dance.

That he might celebrate before the impact, that he might sing the approach
    of the parasites.

A vase may lie for what we think forever in fragments, but a dead man may
    not be reassembled.

You see that it is well that the dead man has to take a break now and then.

A respite from the olde ode that was, like every pleasure, an escape from time.

The illusions of art have been to the dead man both beautiful and tiring.

The dead man adjusts the piano bench, he resets the reed, he tunes the
    drum and marimba, he turns the pegs at fret's end.

The dead man cannot resist the music of the spheres.

2. More About the Dead Man's Olde Ode

We're back, the self and the other self, the dead man alive and the other one
      looking ahead.
Were you anticipating some hully-gully, some hooey, some hanky-panky?
The dead man has had to forgo certain pleasures because of the war.
If you ask which war, take your pick or wait for it.
War is the newsy part of the ode, part of the olde ode and part of the new.
The dead man has been increasingly absorbed by elsewhere and others, he is
      one of them.
The body politic suffered, but the missing arms and legs did not stop him.
Even the cruelest head wounds could not stop the dead man from thinking.
So the dead man apologizes for appearing to celebrate wartime, for he
      does not.
It was inescapable that pleasure kept on throughout and between the wars,
      and there were many.
The wars were as constant as lawnmowers in the cemeteries.
In time, the dead man no longer pushed the life force into the face of death.
He had become the first patient, he had perfected the wait-and-see.
He had learned, he had looked it up, he had lived through.
The dead man listens for the sounds of involuntary joy.
He hears the treaties shrivel while children laugh in the yard.
He feels the tremor underneath the long lines of laborers and follows the
      weary to the tavern after work.
So long as there can be a few last drops, the dregs, the bottom of the barrel,
      a sip, a taste, a bite, a sniff of the apple, for that long can time-to-come
      retain its welcome.
The dead man's ode was always about the planet and the dance.
It was always about the collapse of empires.
It was always about the silvery cloud edge that winked as it reshaped itself.
He who would last awhile must sprinkle himself widely among all that is not
      himself, you odists listen.

The Book of the Dead Man (*Kiss Kiss*)

1. About the Dead Man (*Kiss Kiss*)

The dead man is of the future, but he will not breathe a word of it.

The dead man will say he is the patchwork offspring of Mother Nature and
　　Father Time.

He frames it thus when folksy, as others say *tsk tsk* to youth or *kiss kiss*
　　for goodbye.

He is common, even so he has tried to pry official fingers from the nuclear
　　button.

He is common, even so he has tried to smoke out the cranks.

The dead man has seen his nation shoot itself in the foot with a blood lust
　　for guns.

He has seen it smoke itself to death.

He has lived among the wistful who can only rub a brass lamp.

He has boarded with the fry cook and the pool tender, the taskmaster and
　　the idler.

He doesn't wear a suit, he is small-town, common, he is one-at-a-time.

2. More About the Dead Man (*Kiss Kiss*)

Where now a cyclotron spirals particles at Brookhaven National Laboratory,
     there was Camp Upton.
The dead man saw the soldiers mustering out.
He was a child among the khaki strap undershirts, buffeted by the
     commotion at the edge of imminent release.
This was the old way of war, one tour of duty and a discharge.
The dead man's father drove to the camp to hire a veteran.
And there were prisoners, then, working at roadsides or in fields, happy to
     have been pulled from the fighting.
And the veterans of older wars who said nothing afterward.
The dead man is a veteran of an army rent by the hubris of empire.
Now dead men and dead women live among the bereaved of war, live and
     pass away, live and pass away.
The dead man dies with the fallen soldier and the aged veteran equally.

The Book of the Dead Man (Light Skeleton)

1. About the Dead Man and the Light Skeleton

What if the dead man were a skeleton with wings?

Black and white, an inflatable skin without blood, no gristle, no spiky relays,
    no stretchy tendons.

Picture him having shed his inner organs.

He is light now, he can hover, he can temper your fear with a sense of floating.

There is, on the one hand, a bucket of heavy innards, and on the other, there
    is the unexpected lightness of the dead man.

He enters in a whiteness more white than white, a doorway to the sun.

Only look up to see him.

It seems he entered your consciousness without tripping the alarm.

He moved past the watchdogs, who remain silent.

It is a whiteness more white than a cessation of thought.

2. More About the Dead Man and the Light Skeleton

The butterfly was too small, the hummingbird too quick, the nightingale too
    rare, it took the dead man.

It was a blinding light, a white glass to the past, a life in midair.

From the sun spreading, from cinders flying, from the whistle of skeleton
    bones, the dead man may enter.

As from a line of gull song screaming, he may suddenly beach.

From a ripple back of the bricks, from a wisp on high, from the poppies
    puckering, from unwavering resolve, he may be born.

What if he comes bearing the rib cage of starvation and a cape?

He may enter as an irrational surge of current.

He may be too large for the space allotted him, and take the air.

He may be the parade balloon you hoped had escaped.

The dead man adds bounce to the hours, and he stays up.

The Book of the Dead Man (The Metronome)

1. About the Dead Man and the Metronome

The dead man's straight shot is a jagged path from the surface, a sawtooth
    descent, a switchback of expectations.
They will be making lemonade out of lemons, or so they say.
They will ululate as the dead man passes, they will hurry at a good clip
    behind the body, they may rattle their bracelets and key rings.
They do this after each assassination, too.
For now, the dead man has merely closed the metronome, folded the
    triangle and unwound the clock.
The dead man, as an insider, thought like an outsider.
He is a kind of Klein bottle, a sort of human Möbius strip.
He was not schooled in beauty.
He was not swaddled in entitlement or posh classrooms.
He just had a tic for looking around the corner like the double-jointed fans
    of superheroes.
Of course he has the powers of prescience and prophecy, who doesn't?
He saw early that space eats time, and he moved to the periphery.
The dead man is a fringe element.

2. More About the Dead Man and the Metronome

The dead man quit the jamboree at the point of congestion.
He could not see from far inside the populace.
He avoided the group singing, the book lists, his own first opinions.
He made light of the flap over who matters and what counts.
He will leave in his wake a budding new music hovering in synapses.
The dead man's metronome is irregular, the regular one was remedial.
He doubles the stresses of, "Give me your tired, your poor."
Because his government has stopped listening.
The elected took piano lessons, they learned to count, they tapped their feet.
Then they took down a nation by the numbers.
The dead man thinks our minorities will save us from them.
Where there are too many of them, there are too few of us.
The dead man hears in the metronome the sound of hubris.
The dead man proclaims an elastic measure only some can follow.

The Book of the Dead Man (Mount Rushmore)

Washington, Jefferson, T. Roosevelt, Lincoln

1. About the Dead Man and Mount Rushmore

To become the face of a mountain—you'd think he'd want it.
To be the high cheekbones on high, the forehead that bedevils the crowd
　　with its façade of knowing.
But the dead man hears the crowing of the birds, who alight without a
　　semblance of symbolism or accolades.
Yet if the dead man should lie prone, he, too, may be lifted over eons to
　　a peak.
He, too, may be thrust into the heavens.
If, that is, he is not slowly lowered into the simmering core of a mountain-
　　making workshop.
Let him look now at the great faces being groomed by weather.
Let him climb hand-over-hand with a toothpick in his mouth and a cap
　　jaunty for the thrill.
No president shall fall from this perch, he thinks.
The dead man would like to bring back the earthly versions of these four.
To set them at the doors to the latest presidential libraries with torches in
　　their hands.
To coat the war criminals with the slime of their origins, to spit boulders at
　　the Congress.
It is, the dead man thinks, a long way down from these four.
Their faces were lifted, who would never have sanctioned a face-lift.
Their visages were blasted clean, who were men with dirt under their nails.
Their sixty-foot heads went on whispering beneath the shroud placed by
　　John Fire Lame Deer of the Lakota.
They went on whispering, the dead man could hear it, they debated what
　　is necessary, what is inescapable, what is random and what can be
　　forgiven.

The dead man can hear atonements so slight they only bend the fire reeds
in wind.
He can sense apologies so tentative they murmur only when the brook runs.

2. More About the Dead Man and Mount Rushmore

To the argument over who was anyplace first, the dead man offers himself.
For he is made of particles that came from the near and far, from the creek
bed and the seven wonders of the ancient world.
The dead man knows the quantum means that you cannot fix him.
So here, he thinks, is the visible difference.
Here on this Rushmore is the chiseled perpetuity to which mankind looks up.
Yet the dead man is of another stripe, another streak, another vein, another
lode and deposit, not to be recovered in toto.
You'd think he'd want it, to be of the earth itself, but of course he will be.
Without his wanting to.
There will be another tectonic uplifting, count on it.
The dead man can feel a spasm so deep it is recorded only when a needle
shudders on graph paper.
Here come, reborn, the stone Cheyenne and the stone Lakota.
Here come the displaced, here come the rabble.
The dead man is in the way, here come the warriors on horseback.
The dead man knows that the victorious will win by any means.
He can hear the long rue, he can hear the late regret, he can hear the apologies
so undermined by monuments that they surface out of reach.
They are in the air, they are weightless, they are shadows the sun permits
when it chooses.
Up he goes with wonderment and a loose tooth.
Up he goes with sore knees and a locked trigger finger.
Up he goes without piety where the stone-faced have been sentenced to look
straight ahead.

The Book of the Dead Man (Movie Theater)

1. About the Dead Man and the Movie Theater

The dead man has been reading subtitles in the dark.
They leave out some anatomy, they cut the cussing.
He looks up and down to see the figures on the screen, who are larger than
     their words.
He tries to follow the players as they persist in their visions.
One of them wants to go straight, another seeks revenge.
The dead man has seen too much, now he hopes the lovers don't fight.
Likewise, he prefers those who are still coming of age to get there.
The dead man thinks their speech contains the seeds of its destruction.
The cold subtitles mute their passions.
The scene morphs, the light shifts, the seats creak, all of it safely.

2. More About the Dead Man and the Movie Theater

The dead man returns to the dark magic of the movie theater.
A sensitivity to light blankets the room as the house lamps dim.
The red Exit signs slide farther into the dead man's peripheral vision.
From high up, the projector sends a tide of light overhead, a river of slivers
     that reassemble at the silver screen.
Now the dead man is emptied of foreknowledge.
The film begins, there may be foreshadowing, flashback, time shifts.
The theater swells with points of view.
Let him last through the credits at the end, blinking as he wakes.
To the dead man, every movie is a home movie he is privy to.
He is the eye behind the camera, he is a mystery to the characters.
They are not themselves, they pretend he cannot see them.

The Book of the Dead Man (The Northwest)

And the fish swim in the lake
and do not even own clothing.

Ezra Pound, "Salutation"

1. About the Dead Man and the Northwest

Picture the dead man in two rooms in the northwest corner of his being.
In the one, it is day, and in the other, night, and he lives in both.
His street dead-ends at a cliff above a rattling of ropes clanging on masts
     and the whimper of lazy tides.
There are lumps on the sea bottom.
There is also, as elsewhere, a worldly stomping that threatens the scale pan
     of justice.
The dead man fingers a lucky stone like Casanova his address book.
For the Northwest, which may feel ashen to the displaced Easterner under
     the white of a winter sky, pleases him greatly.
It is the density of forest that overwhelms his language, as the dexterity of
     the tides smooths his hours and the mountain passes frame the light
     at midday.
The dead man smells the faint fizz of froth at shore's edge.
It is the smell of the soap the adolescent rinses away before a date.
It is the loamy feel in his throat when a young man is asked to speak.
The dead man has opened the map, and run his finger along the interstates,
     and driven west to land's edge.
The dead man's distant friends look toward England, it is old.
The dead man is himself old but is forever newly at home.
He who grew up near the sunrise feels more at home near the sunset.
That's the dead man's duality, drawn east-to-west and south-to-north.

2. More About the Dead Man and the Northwest

Though we make a junkyard of the sea, still the fish wink.
The dead man's turf is piled with lug nuts and vinyl, tubing and wire, razor
　　　blades, batteries, bubble wrap and book bags—name anything.
Still the dead man toasts both the present and the absence to come.
Salmon that went against the current.
Madrones that peeled without a whimper, you seers take notice.
The dead man has a favorite heron because they see one another daily.
And the one sits in the other's tree and squawks when it flies off or returns.
What makes one go here or there, and stay, may be the rhythm of the heart,
　　　or the firing of brain cells or the feel of the air.
The dead man has heavy bones, he does not float.
He has small pores.
He cannot be smelled as quickly by the wolf, a trait that brought them face
　　　to face.
He walks by the elk and the deer who do not care.
Like them, he knows time by the look of the light and the smell.
The dead man, standing between the Pacific and Cascades, at the tip of the
　　　Quimper Peninsula, is almost out of time.
The dead man is not as much about *doing*.
The dead man was, and will be, and, for now, just is.

The Book of the Dead Man (Nothing)

1. About the Dead Man and Nothing

The dead man knows nothing.

He is powerless to stop the battles, he has no way to reattach the arms
and legs.

He cannot stuff the fallen soldier's insides back inside.

He has no expertise in the matter of civilian corpses, nor of friendly fire, nor
beheadings, nor revenge, nor suicide.

He does not know the depth of depth charges, or the exact pressure that
detonates a land mine.

The dead man has given his all so that now, if he once knew, he knows
nothing.

He is emptied, he is the resonant cavity of which he spoke when it was
music he was thinking of.

Let him be now the leftover button of his work shirt.

Permit him his fading mirror, his sputtering circuits, his secrets, his tears,
his noonday duels with the sun.

Let him ride the roads in the bucket of an earth mover, can it hurt?

Let him stand under the icicles, can he catch cold?

For the dead man is stagnant without knowledge, and he cannot survive the
demise of philosophy or art.

To the dead man they were not spectacles, but survival skills.

To the dead man, the world was but a birthmark that befell original space.

To say that the dead man knows nothing is to see him at the beginning, who
can it hurt?

Before all this, he was nothing.

2. More About the Dead Man and Nothing

Don't bet he won't be born.
Before all this, this that is so much, he was not himself.
He was the free heat of space and then the salt of the earth.
He was the ring around the moon, foretelling.
The dead man had no station when he came to be, just a strange nakedness
     in the light.
He did not know what he was to do, this was before clocks.
So he decided to stab the dirt, to tumble in happiness and writhe in pain,
     and to flap his way into space.
To go home.
It was a swell idea for the dead man, and he pinned it to his chest.
Give him that, that he crystallized a plan, that he made from smoke
     something to him as real as quartz, ivory, or the hoof of a gelding.
The dead man had the whole world to transform or perfect or outlive.
He wrote the book of nothing and no-time that entombed all time and all
     that took place in time.
The dead man could not be hammered by analysis.
Let him horn in on your fury, whatever it was, and it will abate.
The energy that became form will disperse, never again to be what we were.
Look out the window to see him, no, the other one.

The Book of the Dead Man (The Nuclear Submarine)

1. About the Dead Man and the Submarine

Earlier, the dead man fired the mortar and bazooka, lobbed the grenade and
    swept the barrel of the automatic.
He boarded the troop copter, the armored carrier, the jeep.
He shouldered the rifle and wore the night revolver on duty.
He was called out when the AWOL soldier lay down on the railroad track.
He kept his head down on the infiltration course.
He shared his foxhole, his rations, his canteen.
He was not brave, he was one of the boys, he would have gone along if called.
Those dead man days shrink aboard the nuclear sub, touring its armament,
    its math and physics, its dark genius.
It takes two grips to fix a bayonet but only fingers to launch an atom bomb.
The dead man descended to the lower decks where the gauges were masked.

2. More About the Dead Man and the Submarine

The crew moved quicker, not stepping but sliding down the vertical ladders
    with a whoosh.
The crew that slept on mattresses between the missiles.
The crew that worked in colored lamplight before a puzzle of gauges.
The crew that loses its depth of field to each six months at sea.
The crew members listening but never transmitting, their location the
    captain's secret.
And the torpedoes longer than a string of limos at the ready.
In the labyrinth below the waterline, a network of interdependence, call it a
    warren, a burrow, a den, a lair.
Call it reliance, call it trust, call it faith.
The dead man, like you, wants to be safe, but is not.
The dead man, like you, is in the sights, on the target, inside the zone,
    acceptably collateral, and a man on a mission.

The Book of the Dead Man (The Numbers)

1. About the Dead Man and the Numbers

The dead man is outside the pale.

The dead man makes space for himself the way a soccer player moves to the place to be next.

The angles shift, the pace slows and picks up, it matters more, then less, then more, then less, and others run by in both directions.

One of them may slow to stoke the embers of a failing thought.

For example, the dead man restores the poet's ambition to plumb the nature of existence.

Sometimes he, sometimes she, asks the dead man what it is to live as if one were already dead.

It's the feel of an impression in the earth, a volume in space, an airy drift upward.

It's downwind and upwind at the same time.

It's a resonance to wrap one's mind around, like a bandage beneath which the healing may happen.

It's the idea of turf beyond the neighborhood.

It's a cold flame in a hot season.

It's what you do facing the guns.

2. More About the Dead Man and the Numbers

Here we go, with what it takes.

The dead man wakes in a dream, lungs aching as if the night were a stairway
    or a hill.

Is he indoors or out, an insider in public or an outsider at home?

He hears a splash of tissue in a knee and a click as his shoulder slips the edge
    of an obstruction.

You would think he thinks himself awake, but the dead man does not.

He has a way of making the ephemeral last, the rusting slow, the leaf hang,
    the bullet hold up in midair.

In the waking world, there are too many of us to tell, the ushers are
    overwhelmed by the numbers wanting a box seat.

The preacher offering a future world, the historian waxing nostalgic, and the
    dead man underwriting them is what it takes.

How is it to be the dead man among shifting loyalties?

It means living in the interstices, swimming in the wake of the big boats,
    crossing the borders on back roads.

It means taking the field with those whose lives are numbered.

It means finding space for when it will matter.

The Book of the Dead Man (Orchards)

1. About the Dead Man and the Orchards

The dead man walks among apples and oranges.

He favors each in its time.

He has had, for some long time, little in common with the prudes and prunes.

With the cross, flush-faced, trembly handed, antiplay, windy, laced-up,
     unwild, odorous defenders of poetic retrograde.

Notwithstanding, let us yet honor the past and cotton to its iambic civilities.

The dead man is a metrician in disguise and a wild man in a mask.

Let the hour come when he finds himself at the edge, and still he will not
     satisfy your cravings for a talky why.

Or for toys.

His laughter, existential and absurdist, will linger for you when the little
     billy club jokes have gone their way.

You see a bowl of fruit on a table and think what?

An invitation to make art?

Or do you see again, as does the dead man, your father picking fruit for
     pennies—if he told you.

When the dead man was barely a child, he remembered that he did not try
     to remember.

The white porcelain of the boys' urinal was to him an early blank page.

This is true, he does not recall his childhood but for the feelings.

He was not afraid, he was sometimes afraid, he was always afraid.

In his father's house there were many rooms, and places under the beds, and
     room in the closets, and an attic like a kerchief over it all.

The dead man took survival training without leaving home.

2. More About the Dead Man and the Orchards

The dead man prolongs the memory of an immigrant father.
He recalls a father who ran the trenches to drag off the dead, it was the old
      country, it was long ago.
That is why he is the dead man, that and the future.
The dead man remembers, too, the eleven horses cresting the hill as he
      walked toward them through the buffalo sod.
That memory is his own, he didn't make it up, it apes the recent past.
From such outings does pleasure pleasure, as a bite of a wild apple may
      open the day.
To the dead man, the planet is an orchard of the whole.
He seeks the play of fruit scent in the wind, he edges by the hour toward the
      earth that trembles but is not afraid.
The dead man wrote in an age of handmade lace which passed for an
      artifact of true nature.
He wrote in a time of inverted bowls, of minds unable to bear the cross,
      but wept the red tears of the guilty survivor.
He heard them say, "hot damn," "cool cat."
He stayed up late to sing and dance—alone.
Nothing better embodies the human condition than the dead man.
He has the fermentation on his skin, the same.
He is the picker, he is the accountant, he weighs the baskets.
It was a good thing there were horses.
They let his father ride at night too far for the guards to see him gone.
It was the orchard that fed him, now it is the dead man who nourishes the
      orchard for next time.

The Book of the Dead Man (The Palm)

1. About the Dead Man and the Fortune-Telling Palm

The dead man lives with omens, tentative forecasts, strict calculations,
     guesses and earnest prophecies.
Also, estimations, conjectures, projections, the weight of statistics and the
     drift of hope.
Those who know the dead man are beside themselves with contradictions,
     what to say and from which self?
For he is here and not here, as it will be foretold after he has gone.
There was the famous cat in a box, and the quantum cat, which is a way of
     looking at the cat without seeing it.
It is not enough that space is curved, even a fly's eyes see only a little.
Now comes the panorama of the lifeline, the health line, the head line
     and fate.
It isn't easy, and he drinks coffee.
It isn't easy, and his fingers hurt from striking the keys.
It isn't a snap, and his wrists crackle when he waves or beckons.

2. More About the Dead Man and the Fortune-Telling Palm

In the second act of the play, the statues decided to work.
They stepped off their pedestals to become like us, common hands.
The dead man's hands fit the crown of his head.
They can cup a knee or cover his ears or muffle his speech.
Go to the fortune-teller with your hands behind your back.
Go to the wise man with an empty mind.
Holding up his hands in front of his eyes, the dead man sees the mounts of
     Venus and Luna.
He sees himself holding love and the night, and his fate is in his hands, too.
He wills himself to flatten his hands, one against the other, it isn't easy.
It isn't easy, and he doesn't pray.

The Book of the Dead Man (The Pause)

Marcelo Lucero, b. 1971–d. Nov. 8, 2008
Patchogue, New York

1. About the Dead Man and the Pause

Seven young men went looking to beat up a Hispanic and found one and
    killed him, and the dead man will speak of it.
The dead man pauses to consider, to ruminate, to extrapolate, to ponder, to
    chew over, to digest.
He knows they wanted to stop the world, who fell in warfare.
He knows they wanted to stop time, who faced the guns.
The seven who stabbed to death a stranger wanted to stop their anger but
    could not.
The dead man has to be a dead man to make it stop.
He has to take stock, which takes time, time that is ravaged by entropy.
The dead man has invented God.
God is the filling-in of the blanks, the filling-up of the cavities and wounds,
    the words that blanket the cold, the eyes looking, the body expectant,
    the one chance in a million.
The dead man has also invented the inner life.
The inner life is the re-creation of the young Ecuadorian knifed to death in
    Patchogue just days before the invention of the inner life.
The inner life is the rebirth of the young Marine sharpshooter who a week
    earlier was memorialized by renaming a bridge.
The inner life, the inner life . . . is no escape.
So the dead man has invented the pause, which is God, which is the
    inner life.
Such small particles may float free from any action that a dead man may die
    again, or live again, seen only by the few who pause to consider.
It was the dead man who said that the purpose of life was to look out
    the window.

What window, what perch, what time, what self?

The dead man is halfway up the ladder, or is coming down.

The dead man has less self than the newsworthy, less ego than the
sophisticate, less purchase than the wealthy.

The dead man will not sell his secrets, nor tattle.

Many others must know before the dead man will admit that he knows, too.

2. More About the Dead Man and the Pause

The dead man abides in the pauses, in the gaps, the interstices, the breaches,
    the slits, the fissures, the chasms, the in-betweens and not-yets.
Picture a clock one can reach to turn back the hands.
Picture a handkerchief not yet folded.
The dead man opens again the wound of the victim.
When the dead man, kneeling by the body, tries to stand, he becomes
    nauseated.
Because the dead man is you, was always you, he tallies the crimes you
    know from the papers, they are local.
Here is the slaying of last week, and the one from last night, and the map of
    neighborhoods coded for killings.
The dead man set out to speak of the one crime, the one whose face is on
    page 1.
The dead man tore the seven bullies in half, he could not resist.
He kept alive the picture of the slain, while he crumpled the defense lawyers
    who have no case but their fees.
Such nice haircuts, such well-fit new suits, and the defendants sit still, too.
If they choose not to testify, well, the dead man will use their silence
    against them.
The dead man wanted to write poetry, but the streets were blocked.
The way forward was too loud, too fraught, it was a rebuke to the
    applications of beauty.
The dead man can't see straight, it's you again.
The dead man wanted to write about it, but police tape kept him away.
The dead man is leaving it to you, what are you going to do?
If the sun came out, if the handkerchief remained in the hip pocket, if the
    clock was on time, if the fire siren only meant lunch, if the ambulance
    did not have to drive on the shoulder, if the fatalities ran down to zero,
    the dead man would be comical.
The dead man has heard the jokes about Saint Peter.
The dead man invented God, he invented the inner life, they were easy.
Heaven is harder.

The Book of the Dead Man (Peacetime)

1. About the Dead Man in Peacetime, If and When

If and when the war is over, the dead man's days will seem longer.

When the ammo is spent, the funds discharged, when the fields have shut
down and the flares fallen, an hour will take an hour.

Time for the dead man lengthens when the shooting stops.

The waiting for the next war to begin can seem endless, though it take but a
week, a month or a year.

The low intensity conflicts, the raids and assassinations, the deployments
and withdrawals, the coups and revolutions, the precursors and
aftermaths—it's a lifetime of keeping track.

It's as if the sun fell and fizzled—somewhere.

Then the black, white and gray propaganda, the documents planted on
corpses, the reading of tea leaves and bones . . .

The dead man takes stock in the darkness of peacetime.

The Judas goats stand waiting in the corrals.

We are the sheep that gambol through dreamless nights.

A quietude hangs in the air, an expectancy, the shimmer that some believe
presages alien life forms.

The calm before the stampede.

It was wartime when love arrived, yes, love.

It was wartime when the virtuosi performed, standing on their heads, as it
were, for peacetime is our upside-down time.

2. More About the Dead Man in Peacetime, If and When

On a field of armed conflict, in the midst of rushing water, at the lip of a
    canyon, by the border of a fire-torched desert, in the overdark of a rain
    forest, where else was there ever but here?
Do you think poetry is for the pretty?
Look up and down, then, avoiding the hillocks that hold the remains.
The dead man, too, sees the puffy good nature of the clouds.
He welcomes, too, the spring blooming that even the grass salutes.
The dead man has made peace with temporary residence and the eternal
    Diaspora.
Oh, to live in between, off the target, blipless on the radar, silent on the sonar.
To keep one's head down when the satellites swoop over.
Not even to know when the last war is reincarnated and the next one
    conceived.
The dead man sings of a romantic evening in the eerie flickering of the
    last candle.
He whistles, he dances, he writes on the air as the music passes.
It was in wartime that the dead man conceived sons.
The dead man lifts a glass to the beauties of ruin.
The dead man is rapt, he is enveloped, he is keen to be held.

The Book of the Dead Man (Puzzle)

1. About the Dead Man and the Puzzle

In a fat chair by a window, with a mug of coffee, the dead man puzzles.
He who was asked where is beauty sits in its presence.
The color blue is beautiful to him, and the blues, and the black and white of
    a musical score.
The dead man dislikes the color red on politicians, though he likes red hair,
    red horses and red-blooded dissent.
It's a puzzle, what people like, and the dead man is dumbstruck to tally
    the voting.
The dead man trusts Occam's razor to shave the excess, but where is a
    barber fit to be president?
The dead man has seen governments take their star turns while the suffering
    continued backstage.
It is a puzzle at the window that the workers go forth as always.
It is a puzzle that the mugging continues.
He has seen the protesters baptized by water cannon and small arms fire.
He has seen the faces pressed against the gap-toothed gate of the
    presidential mansion.
He has seen the protesters thrash about at a distance and go home.
Beauty, then, is, where else, in the mind's eye, recollected in tranquility.
So, in the autumn of the year 2008, beauty is a puzzle, just that.
Beauty is a helpless bias, is it not?
And the grape was beautiful that the dead man changed into water.

2. More About the Dead Man and the Puzzle

The dead man puzzles out the planetary system.
Caught in the political orbit, he assembles an aggregate of minorities.
The dead man has fit together mankind's wish to do good with mankind's
   wish to do well and the explosion of rampant capitalism.
The dead man is a dinner guest with much on his plate.
Say it again, the dead man is dumbstruck.
Say it once more, the dead man is puzzled, all at sea, baffled but not
   bamboozled.
The dead man works the green puzzles of the earth, the white puzzles of
   the poles, the blue puzzles of the sky and oceans, the orange puzzle of
   the setting sun, the yellow puzzle of the pollen, the red puzzle of the
   bloodstream.
It has been the dead man's fate to know and yet be puzzled.
It has taken all this time to be startled.
Just as it has taken these years of entropy to be raised from the living.
The dead man provokes no envy, for he has left you everything.
The dead man who peered from the gaps in the grapevines.
The dead man who spoke to the man-face in the moon.
He has mugged his way through the illusions of passage, winged it among
   the interrogators, uttered the rash idea after long thought.
He has honed and honed Occam's razor.
At the end, it was the unmiraculous mint that refreshed him where he lay
   taking increasingly shallower breaths.

The Book of the Dead Man (Radio)

1. About the Dead Man and Radio

How best might the dead man organize the signals from multiple receivers?
The dead man's pal has been out counting alien transmissions.
And many of his friends are awaiting the next life, whether soon or well
    down the reincarnation road.
The air is filled with oscillations.
The tuning fork at the center of the universe is fully aquiver.
The phenomenal is personal, ever more so.
The team was locked down in the hotel before the big game.
We have the clotheshorse, we have fitness, we have advertising, we have
    candy and infection.
We live with godsends and bad luck.
The dead man spots the pitfalls in perfection.
He has teammates down the field and farther out in space.
He has pacifist friends in the military and assassins in his Rolodex.
It's tricky to climb the ladder while wearing the tool belt.
It's human to think one knows where the portal is.
It's scientific to measure the infinite.
The dead man best expresses the alternating current, the modulations, the
    morphing and segues.
The dead man is syntax, the dead man is whole, the dead man's sentences last.
He hears the voices overlapping in the air, the signals folding into one
    another, the circumnavigational layering.
He listens to the call-in shows of the past.
He hears the pages crackling as the news of the day is rebroadcast.
A cacophony of harmonics and parasitics overlays the airwaves.
The dead man is happy among aliens and outsiders, he favors the party
    favors that make noise.

2. More About the Dead Man and Radio

After the long warm-up, the dead man mustered the stamina to begin again.
If you, reader, cannot take another step, the dead man understands.
If you want finality, one-piece art, a never changing document.
The dead man's portrait changes according to atmospheric pressure, and he
      has been known to grimace when others are laughing and laugh when
      others are earnest.
It was a corporate disadvantage not to fit in, but he lives elsewhere.
There was lingo on both sides of the beat oscillator, look it up.
There was meaning in the shrugs, the grunts and screams, the giggles
      and yelps.
Why not life as it is instead of these artifacts?
The dead man was shaped by radio, by ear, by temperature and static.
It was radio radiating and the phases of the moon.
The dead man is of the invisible world that is itself material.
Keep the little whistle in your pocket, it will be handy.
And a flashlight for the cemetery, the stones wear away.
When the flag flutters, when the tide slaps the shore, when the car tires send
      up a hum during rush hour, that's radio.
It was radio when the dead man's ears flared.
It was radio loosed the dead man's imagination.
It was the wire recorder, the single-track tape player, the homemade drums,
      it was sound waves that struck him.
Now the rooftops are antennas, the drainpipes resonate, the air is awash in
      signals, the dishes on the sides of homes will be collecting a flood of
      sound scraps.
The dead man learned to listen to the one among many.
Now the dead man is surrounded, blanketed, stirred-in to the seething stew
      of a universe of eternal radio.
For the dead man, as for you, some words are internal, try *milk,* try *dress,*
      try, for the dead man, *radio.*
First listen, then know.

The Book of the Dead Man (The Red Wheelbarrow)

1. About the Dead Man and "The Red Wheelbarrow"

The dead man has been asked about a red wheelbarrow.
Not an actual wheelbarrow, not the thing itself.
The dead man has been asked about the thought of the barrow.
Not of a pushcart, not of the gardener, not of the farmer.
This red wheelbarrow sits pristine after rain.
The dead man can tell it is spring and all, it's the rain.
The dead man, stopping at the Williams home, read the medical shingle.
He did not take down the shingle and carry it to the classroom.
He did not bring the wheelbarrow to school.
Later, the dead man took *Spring & All* to Spain, the one book only.
He had time there to let the little wheelbarrow sit unused.
Thus did the dead man restore the dance of the red wheelbarrow.
Thus did he peel the layers of claptrap.
The dead man flexes his muscles, peels his eyes, licks his lips, sniffs briefly
    and opens his ears.
Then he takes the handles of the red wheelbarrow.

2. More About the Dead Man and "The Red Wheelbarrow"

The dead man hears them talking of "The Red Wheelbarrow."

He hears Williams repeat, "The word is not the thing."

To the dead man, the poem is itself, a dance, a complex of the sensory at a distance neither of time nor of space.

Albeit, it is as well a piece in a jigsaw of the imagination and a credo born of desire.

The dead man hath interred in the classroom the canon.

The dead man does not cease his dancing to name the tune.

The dead man places the red wheelbarrow next to a red wagon, in the garage with the silver roller skates, near a scooter made from a vegetable crate.

It is so clean, this unreal wheelbarrow, wetted, waiting, sacramental.

The dead man can hold in mind a red wheelbarrow and a blue guitar at the same time.

They are equally light in the ether.

Stevens was music, Williams was dance, the wheelbarrow was red.

The dead man rode the wheelbarrow and picked the guitar.

The dead man heard the music of the spheres even as he felt, also, the dance of the galaxies.

The dead man need not defend his turf, for he has drawn no boundary.

So much depended on the poem having no title.

The Book of the Dead Man (Rhino)

1. About the Dead Man and the Rhino

The dead man rode a rhino into Congress.
An odd-toed ungulate in the Congress, and no one blinked.
It was the lobbyist from Hell, the rhino that ate Tokyo, a lightning strike in
    their dark dreams.
A ton of megafauna, and nowhere for a senator to hide.
I'm gonna get you, says the momentum of a rhino.
The rhino has been said to stamp out fires, and the dead man hopes it is true.
He steered the beast to the hotheaded, the flaming racist, the fiery pork-
    barreler, the sweating vestiges of white power.
The dead man's revolutionary rhino trampled the many well-heeled
    lawmakers who stood in the way.
He flattens the cardboard tigers, he crushes the inflated blowhards, he
    squashes the cupcakes of warfare.
Oh, he makes them into blocks of bone like those of compacted BMWs.

2. More About the Dead Man and the Rhino

The dead man's rhino was not overkill, don't think it.
He was, and is, the rough beast whose hour had come round at last.
The dead man's rhino did not slouch, but impaled the hardest cases among
    the incumbents.
The committee chair who thought a rhino horn an aphrodisiac found out.
The dead man's rhino came sans his guards, the oxpeckers.
He was ridden willingly, bareback, he did not expect to survive, he would
    live to be a martyr.
The rhino's horn, known to overcome fevers and convulsions, cleared, for a
    time, the halls of Congress.
The senators who send other people's children into battle fled.
They reassembled in the cloakroom, they went on with their deal-making.
They agreed it takes a tough skin to be a rhino.

The Book of the Dead Man (The River)

1. About the Dead Man and the River

The dead man stands on the bank of a river that overcame its banks.

He stands where the river has made a new road to ride.

He strides the shore and salutes the ones in boats looking to help, the
homeowners returning in rubber boots, and the store owners who
carried their inventory on their backs.

He pictures the convoy of artworks spirited away by night to the big city.

He doffs his cap to the sandbaggers and the boxers of books, and to those
whose signatures can float a loan.

The dead man earlier hath seen the river complacent, he hath stopped it in
time, he hath likened it to the curve of space.

He hath seen in it the impenetrability of time.

And if he must swallow hard nature's indifference, still the story was always
about the planet, never about us.

Now he must witness the depth to which thinkers go not to say so.

Here is the mud so full of life forms, and now the river makes a deposit and
backs away and makes another and turns and makes another and so on.

The dead man is bigger than the river only because he lives as if he is dead.

He is greater than the planet only because he lives as if he is pure energy.

What size shirt and cape fit a man of pure energy?

Does he wear galoshes or waders, does he stand on the water or slumber on
the bottom, is he human?

The dead man stopped asking when he eased the separation between here
and there, now and then, land and sea, angst and regret.

The dead man's life is about what is happening.

2. More About the Dead Man and the River

The dead man does not hold still for his portrait.

He stands at river's edge in a watery wind, as elsewhere he lay on thermal
ground to dispute the horizon.

It was the thunder that crinkled the paper and his picture.

It was the water that erased it, the fire that made ashes of ashes, the air that
carried them off, and the dirt that colored them.

The dead man has found a replacement for the self.

He has absorbed the solitudes that gather in crowds.

He has heeded the alarm of the crow and the bark of the rooster as they
marked out the day.

Now he adopts a posture that pressures the edges of the picture, a bearing
that disperses the one self, a carriage about to go.

How shall he throw out his arms if not akimbo?

How shall he be less than haphazard, less the dumb luck collector, less the
random apocalypse that blinked from another galaxy?

The dead man is faceup to the sun and stars.

He is the longitude and latitude of his whereabouts, the wrinkly motto of his
forehead, the tattoo in the mud attributed to aliens.

The dead man stands for a portrait that is all hello.

What would have been anything without the dead man?

It was history in the making when the dead man first appeared, he is the
reason you turn the picture over to check.

Until the dead man, there was no water under the bridge, there was no past.

The Book of the Dead Man (The Roads)

1. About the Dead Man and the Roads

The dead man has taken both the high road and the low road.

He has traveled enough of the low road to have seen it awash in the liquidity
of the wealthy.

He has seen the waterlines on the houses of the poor who live low for the
rich farmland, the quick fish, the watery appraisals.

Now the dead man must live high, higher than the built-up turnpike, higher
than the bridges, above the condos and roof gardens, above the belfries
and steeples.

He must live above the rooftop water savers and exhaust fans where the
workers struck an American flag in better days.

He must live high to see who is coming.

Not the armies, not the rebels, not the educated rabid nor the dismal who
need to talk, nor the rampant criminal, nor any creature with or
without speech and self-thought.

That's right, the dead man has his head in the clouds.

The dead man knows that to be safe and awake one must be everywhere and
nowhere at once.

This the dead man can accomplish as only a living dead man can.

He looks down now, but not in judgment.

He is not of the critical masses, he is, rather, the first and the last, the here and
the gone, the always and the never, he is fit for lifetimes beyond his own.

Let the man or woman who has perfect knowledge of the zero and has seen
the folly of the one find these writings in the future.

For they are next, not previous, they are ahead not prior, they claim the
territory beyond the sensate, they exceed the last frontier, they go.

2. More About the Dead Man and the Roads

The dead man is on time, though he disputes the notion.

The dead man is the purveyor of a clock face without hands, of a sundial for night, of starry pixels refreshing the sky.

It would be too easy for the dead man to buy into time.

It would be simple to say yes I know what you mean, if he meant it.

The dead man thinks the meaning is not what you mean.

It is not intention, nor success, not standing, not the hammer or the chisel, not the rock face or the river bottom.

It is not where you will go, but where you are.

Were you rash, and are you now rusty, were you sheepish, do you envy the vagabond?

Did you digress to wax nostalgic, and did you wise up?

It is not where you go but what you are.

The dead man likes the high road for its rattling pace, its single-mindedness, its web of isolate sensibilities.

The dead man likes the low road for its backtalk amidst acres of rubble, its überworldly sass, its animal ooze.

He has steered his way across hollows and knolls, on- and off-road, to the spiral exits and the blunt dead ends.

Now he has somewhere to go that isn't on the roads.

The Book of the Dead Man (Scars)

1. About the Dead Man and Scars

There's a shiny scarring on the blade of the scissors where the dead man
    cut copper.
And a scar in the mirror, backward.
Where his elbow opened the door, there's an oval scar.
And a long scar on the cheek of his nemesis from the dream struggle.
There is a thin scar on the plate where the knife sawed too long.
And a scar in his throat just now from the hot soup.
The dead man could go on forever, listing his scars, but there's no time.
If there were time, which there never was, he could draw you a map.
He has scars inside and out, and a rattle in his head.
The dead man flexes his muscles and checks his scars in private.

2. More About the Dead Man and Scars

Outdoors in a dream, the dead man thought he was riding a bull, but it was
    only a gust of wind.
He thought he was hoofing it home, but it was his leg, twitching.
Never mind his nemesis, or his illusions, the dead man has an outlet, which
    is waking.
He wakes from the scarred world of dreams to a water-stained ceiling and
    streaked window glass.
His hand on the blanket is scarred from the time he gunned a motorbike
    downhill.
Oh, the dead man's scars are like bandages.
He is held together by the marked veins and arteries within him.
He waited out the scabs that became scars and scar tissue.
Now he is impenetrable.
Now he can open a door with his elbow and not feel a thing.

The Book of the Dead Man (The Shovel)

1. About the Dead Man and the Shovel

The dead man steps on the shovel that will dig him up.

It's the dance a dead man does, with one foot on a shovel and one foot in the grave.

The dead man is Nijinsky's understudy, he is the janitor at La Scala, he is a stowaway on the freighter.

He is the underside of the surf, where a swimmer, pancaked by a wave, is trying to breathe again.

With his shovel, the dead man digs a shoe and a scarf from the snow.

Is it funny that the dead man fears being buried alive?

He shovels up an earth in which human parts are encased in rectangles, cones and parallelograms.

His is the land rutted by oxen, gritty with crumbled pillars and the torsos of clay gods.

He is a digger of graves, even his own, he is not shy.

You will know him by his spade, his scoop, his ladle, his love of the Big and Little Dippers.

How natural to think him digging, dredging, excavating, hollowing out, gouging, then burrowing.

The dead man is also the wood and pulp, the buried fish and eggshells, all the totemic items sent to the afterlife.

He knows what the revered poet said about his son, and about you.

He knows what is useful and for how long.

2. More About the Dead Man and the Shovel

So now they want the dead man to tell them.

They want the juicy pieces, the drippings, the blood and the tears.

They think he can answer for the Absurd.

They think the dead man has caulked the places from which the hungers
    trickled, so that now nothing more matters.

They think it, because he abandoned distinctions, because he archived
    desire, but it is not so.

If only the dead man had found a dragon to slay, he might have returned us
    to moral zero, that's the myth.

None will know what the dead man whispered to the president with his
    cabinet still in the vestibule.

The dead man is equally the voice of the White House and the dollhouse.

Equally so, the dead man improvises a way to fit in.

Witness him shoveling soil by the magnolia, scooping ashes at the chimney,
    for he goes where the work is.

His loyalty to the present is the icing on the cake of our celebrations.

He is the one who will face off with those of forked tongues, the hurlers of
    brickbats, the professors of quagmire.

The dead man is mythic only because he is not too lofty to sink.

The dead man is not freaky, he is one of us, a shoveler.

The Book of the Dead Man (The Sun)

1. About the Dead Man and the Sun

The dead man has asked material things to speak of the sun.
The dead man is the one who fully embraces the sun.
He loves the throbbing ball of fire.
He feels the water rising to meet it, the earth absorbing it, the air spreading it.
Of the four elements, it is the sun of which he has the most experience and
     the fewest words.
The dead man has been visited in dreams by a fox, it was the sun.
He saw the wolf on the hilltop and the coyote in the valley, it was the sun.
Something like a large weasel crossed his path, it was the sun coating the
     black pelt with color.
The dead man hath unearthed the new words that can bring the sun closer.
He hath opened a bible to the Creation.
He hath walked by the bog and the lake to see the light drawn down and
     returned.
He hath looked into the mirrors of the water, the encapsulating canyon walls
     tanning at dawn, the green flash of sunset at the horizon.
The sun was in his eyes, so what did he see?

2. More About the Dead Man and the Sun

The dead man hears the sun hiss, what is that?

The sun has been personified as the head of an angel, can it be?

It has been thought of as desire, as wisdom, as an eye, as a passenger in
     Apollo's chariot.

All of it true in the lexicon of transcendent metaphor.

For the dead man, too, looks to make something more of the solar system.

He, like you, revolved around the parent, so it is like himself, is it not?

He, too, felt the heat and the light, he, like you, was sometimes blinded.

The dead man, of all men, suffers the poverty of language.

Let the sun sweeten the air beyond capture, let it be too little or too much,
     let it be white at noon and auroras at the poles.

We will know it by the halos of our heroes and heroines, we will see it in the
     sea and snow, we will devour it after harvest.

The dead man has written to the sun without words and without saying why.

The dead man's time has been more than half of the sundial.

He stays up late and later to look for the sun.

The Book of the Dead Man (Superhero)

1. About the Dead Man and Plastic Man

Patrick "Eel" O'Brian, the dead man has been following you.

Like you, he has reached beyond his corporeal origin, that turf of sinkholes.

Like you, he was taught by the inmates of prisons and hospitals and those at
 sea in their heads.

Like you, he thought he could jump out of his body to be free, but he
 wised up.

He made his body more visible and familiar, more malleable, more osmotic,
 more heady and base, more painful, and yes, more plastic.

William James, writing past the threshold of consciousness, merely entered
 the realm of plasticity.

Plastic Man is the model, he of the pop-out eyes and rubbery shoulders, of
 the slingshot, of knots and bows, he the ensemble of the self.

Surely James knew automatic writing was only the perpetual morphing of a
 plastic consciousness.

Like this, like what you are reading, and seeing, and almost thinking.

A poem is about what is happening as you read it.

2. More About the Dead Man and Plastic Man

Patrick "Eel" O'Brian, you became the one who could reach for the moon.
The one who could hold his beloved's hand from afar.
You went straight.
We pictured the twisty road, the switchbacks of a life, the hard breathing in
	the passes, the sweating and the thirst.
We believed in you for thousands of years before you arrived.
The lever and pulley were stopgaps, the wheel and screw were expedient, we
	were on our way.
Later, the twisted stasis of the yogis, the whirl of the Sufis, the immobility of
	the monk were precursors to a new self.
The dead man is your true progeny.
He is the new self that is many.
He is the self defined by more than shape.

The Book of the Dead Man (Vertigo)

1. About the Dead Man and Vertigo

The dead man skipped stones till his arm gave out.
He showed up early to the games and stayed late, he played with abandon,
      he felt the unease in results.
His medicine is movement, the dead man alters cause and consequence.
The dead man shatters giddy wisdoms as if he were punching his pillow.
Now it comes round again, the time to rise and cook up a day.
Time to break out of one's dream shell, and here's weather.
Time to unmask the clock face.
He can feel a tremor of fresh sunlight, warm and warmer.
The first symptom was, having crossed a high bridge, he found he could not
      go back.
The second, on the hotel's thirtieth floor he peeked from the balcony and
      knew falling.
It was ultimate candor, it was the body's lingo, it was low tide in his inner ear.
The third was when he looked to the constellations and grew woozy.

2. More About the Dead Man and Vertigo

It wasn't bad, the new carefulness.

It was a fraction of his lifetime, after all, a shard of what he knew.

He scaled back, he dialed down, he walked more on the flats.

The dead man adjusts, he favors his good leg, he squints his best eye to
     see farther.

No longer does he look down from the heights, it's simple.

He knows it's not a cinder in his eye, it just feels like it.

He remembers himself at the edge of a clam boat, working the fork.

He loves to compress the past, the good times are still at hand.

Even now, he will play catch till his whole shoulder gives out.

His happiness has been a whirl, it continues, it is dizzying.

He has to keep his feet on the ground, is all.

He has to watch the sun and moon from underneath, is all.

The Book of the Dead Man (The Vote)

1. About the Dead Man and the Vote

The dead man was in the crowd when the militia moved in.
You can't know what the dead man who was there knows.
He was told to pipe down, to tread lightly, to wave when the leaders passed
	on their way to the great hall.
He saw the past reemerge from the future, he saw midnight at noon.
If a dead woman is walking on the street after an election and gets shot, is
	that a vote?
And is beauty in the eye of the beholder, or shall we vote?
The candidate still wants to be in office when the Apocalypse comes.
The dead have voted, the injured have voted, those running from the polling
	places have voted, and those awash in placards have voted twice.
The dead man has voted with a pen, with a punch card, with a lever, in ink
	and blood.
If there were more bread, we would not have to run through the sewers
	clutching our ballots.
The dead man has seen the proud fingers of the illiterate, given a vote.
He has stood on line with the gerrymandered, the disenfranchised, the ones
	who walked miles to make a mark, the hopeful and the fearful.
Shall the dead man choose among the old and new oppressors?
Shall he vote for the army, the navy, the palace guard, the elite, those with
	the common touch, the new paradigm or the public statuary?
The dead man and dead woman will be sending absentee ballots.
They are the root and branch, the stem and the leaf of a free society.

2. More About the Dead Man and the Vote

The dead man keeps his powder dry, his lamp turned low, and his eyes on
the sky.

He hears the say-so of change in the breeze, he sees the calligraphic dance of
the reeds, he smells the dust where people ran.

The dead man will speak, and all the dead will speak, for you cannot soap
the mouths of dead men and dead women.

He can smell a cleansing storm coming while there are ashes on his tongue.

The dead man has strung together the unlikely.

The despot never sees it coming, even as the voters throw open the
palace doors.

Now the dead man sits down to a meal of rice and kebabs.

He could be talking to his beloved, to an engineer, to the ghost of Alexander
the Great, it is a muttering under his breath.

The dead man hath disputed every election.

He hath counted the petitions and depositions, he hath tallied the ballots.

He hath seen the final figures approaching zero.

He hath placed a pox on the parties equally, on the candidates equally, on
the party-line masses.

For it is only the independent for whom the dead man will vote.

The dead man does not buy and sell his preferences.

He enlists the chaos, he joins the rabble, he leads the caucus, then leaves.

The dead man is free.

The Book of the Dead Man (Wartime)

1. About the Dead Man in Wartime

The dead man, dead and alive at the same time, joins up.

Being both dead and alive, the dead man has nothing to lose.

The corpses that were kept out of sight of the president turn up in the
newspapers under their red, white and blue blankets.

The unregistered suicides at the front skew the casualty figures.

The number one adds up, the tens, the hundreds and thousands and
hundreds of thousands.

He cannot find enough wheelbarrows for the innards.

His spade is blunted from the digging.

The dead man is not loyal to America but to Americans.

The dead man was Lincoln's nightmare.

The dead man was a good combatant, he obeyed the orders that took place
in the dark.

He ran the straw dummy through with a polished bayonet.

His insignia shone.

When he tore off his gas mask, he said "Yes, sir" through his tears.

In the barracks, he was orderly, pristine.

For it was military to be headlong, then obeisant.

It was martial to be in step, then scattershot behind fields of fire.

His is the timeless courage of the eternal football player, persuaded that the
team can do more if it just wants to.

He is the lie embodied, the youthful will, the life force beheaded.

Okay then, when there is no weaponry sufficient, no final map, no total
casualty, no last report, no one uniform, no happenstance that is not as
deadly as the tracers, then there is no end to it.

The dead man volunteers, he is needed.

2. More About the Dead Man in Wartime

One can take off the uniform, but it lasts forever.

You want the marching song, the rhythmic call-and-response.

No one leaves the army, dead or alive.

There are books.

The books tell you ahead of time how many will die in the first platoon.

They tell you the terrain, the weather, the time of attack, the forces necessary.

They tell you the aftermath of bullets, shrapnel, gasses and chain reactions.

Have you seen the artillery arching over the horizon—it is beautiful.

Have you witnessed the fireballs, heard the bass thuds of the mortars, and
      felt the recoil of the shoulder-held?

Did you wonder what it was like at the target?

Ask the dead man about the unstanched blood, the stench from amputation.

The dead man has carried the base plate of the inaccurate mortar.

He has slung the semiautomatic that is sure to hit something.

He has crouched in the spray of bullets, his finger still on the safety.

He has unpinned the grenade and cocked his arm like a pitcher with
      no target.

He has lobbed death into the distance without knowing where or why.

He has gone to the front and penetrated the lines, it was asked for.

He has rappelled the side of a cliff in a dark philosophical mood, it was
      training.

He has crawled on his belly without looking up.

He is of the infantry, he has a specialty, he is known by his dog tag.

Here are his boots, of a size to envelop two sets of socks.

He does what soldiers do to survive, you don't want to know.

Here, inside the rattling armored troop carrier, is a smuggled family photo.

The dead man touches the horror day and night, why don't you?

He will be going home.

The Book of the Dead Man (Whiteout)

1. About the Dead Man and the Whiteout

In a whiteout, in a gummy fog, the dead man dissociates.

An opaque breeze singes the foliage.

The dead man is himself a whiteout, an erasure, a palimpsest.

Here is not the artificial parchment of a drafting table, this is human skin
    loose on its binding.

You cannot see all of the dead man, nor can he know all of himself.

You see him in a fog under which you think there may be a sea.

You meet him in silhouette, you meet him cauterized by the sun, you reach
    to touch him and your hand goes on through.

The dead man's story is the page left blank, the bullet empty of powder, the
    ax insufficiently honed.

He looks bigger in outline, he gains stature when held in place.

He looks back, then hurries into the fog without a light.

2. More About the Dead Man and the Whiteout

He has been breathing in the air, that's what.

He remembers the look on your face, the lifted eyebrows, the anticipation
    that crossed your brow as he looked back.

Then he was eaten by the whiteout, leaving only an outline.

The dead man is not changing the future, that's what.

It is the last day of ten or the last year of millions, it is the last century or the
    final seconds, the past is disappearing, that's what.

Write it on the bark or the barn, spell it in the leaves, keep it in shadow,
    everywhere is a new page.

The dead man is as polarized by a whiteout as by a blackout.

Now he must wait for it to lift or find the other side.

Here is the dead man in a stupor, in a haze, a man of mist and murk.

He was out walking early when everything went blank.

The Book of the Dead Man (The Writers)

1. About the Dead Man and the Writers

The dead man has been licking envelopes from the past.

The dead man's mouth is full of old glue.

He registers the poets starving for a yes, the option-dollars left behind when a
       writer ran out of material, the trickle of royalties during writer's block.

He lines up the empty wine bottles, the shot glasses, the dead soldiers.

The dead man has made a pinch pot, a kiln god, a clay-footed statue of a
       famous author.

He remembers the young writer who rediscovered the Mayans.

It was the Dadaists had it right, the Surrealists who knew what was what,
       the Mayans, the Incans, the lost scribes of Atlantis.

The young writer thinks someone must have known how.

The young writer is cast out of himself and lives between what he was and
       what he may be.

The dead man and dead woman do the same.

Hence, the dead man ships his writings to the future.

He is still ten thousand fools, all the young writers at once.

He pitches the universe an idea of the sublime.

He opens his Shakespeare, what else? for a playmate.

2. More About the Dead Man and the Writers

The Sumerians had it, the Etruscans, they knew in antiquity what writing
    could be.
In lofts and basements, in woods or city, at the café or the tavern, the young
    writers live between old and new, between recovery and creation.
The dead man advises them to look past the words.
They open their Dante, what else? to feel what it is to be forlorn.
They roll and pitch on the deck of a rudderless self.
Are they self-similar, thousands more fractals of the natural world?
They gather with the like-minded to mimic, rebel and shape-shift.
They hunger for the wisdom of the dead, they fall for fools.
The dead man was one of you.
Like you, he was a part of the workshop in appearance only.
The dead man has gone to bed exhausted from finding words that could
    stay awake.
Then he recovered the Egyptians and Tibetans who wrote about him.
The dead man, like you, still writes into his ignorance.
That, and abandon, are the writerly attributes, but first he had a body.

The Book of the Dead Man (Your Hands)

1. About the Dead Man and Your Hands

Mornings, he keeps out the world awhile, the dead man.

The dead man, without looking, believes what you said of the garden.

He knows the color of a rose is the color of a rose is the color.

He sees the early sky lit by a burn toward which we sidle.

He will take care of you, the dead man will do that.

He will wait for your hair to grow back.

He thinks the things you touched are lucky to be yours.

The dead man knows where to be and where not to be, how he survives.

He is aware, at all times, of your place, your dog, your rug, your roof, your chairs and tables.

Here is his own table, from the basement of the "as is" shop.

The dead man is of this old table, he is of his front and back doors, he is of the tea on the burner and the burner, too, he is.

It cannot stop the dead man, that others have caught on.

The dead man at his worst still looks his best.

2. More About the Dead Man and Your Hands

Nights, he lets in the world, the dead man does it, always.

By any late night, he has lost the need to believe.

The dead man plays a nighttime piano, he blows a nighttime horn, he sings
    more after midnight.

Dead man's music is nighttime, call it earthly, call it planetary.

The dead man feels the high registers heard by animal ears.

He feels the rumbly pedal note struck by redwoods enlarging and tectonic
    plates lurching.

What is it about his hands and your hands, is it the absence of certainty?

He has stirred distinctions into a broth, a soup, a stew, a gravy.

You cannot find yes and no, true or false, in a dead man's soup.

So what if they have caught on, the dead man is out front and stays up later.

Hence, when the dead man maketh eyes, he's gotcha.

He'll care for you, now that he's gotcha, and he hath giveth his hand.

He can't talk about the children if you are going to cry.

The Book of the Dead Man (Zine)

1. About the Dead Man and the Zine

The dead man saw the one *Electronic Poetry Review* begin and end.
Given the start and the finish, the dead man can toggle the first and the final.
For the Internet lasts forever, with Red Skelton and Martha Raye.
With Caruso, with Churchill, with Einstein inbound in sound waves that
    consume the vacuum.
We in our space bubble can hear the past, we can recast it.
The revisions accumulate, invisibly, randomly layered in dimensions beyond
    plane and direction.
We can go now, let's say, to the end point of each war.
We can see for ourselves the carnage morph into the bodies before they
    were shredded.
The dead man has all of his faculties, and can smell and hear those times of
    what is fondly called "yore."
The dead man, like others, must live in it and squeak.
When the dead man advises poets to stop whining, they hear it wrong and
    think it means to stop drinking.
The dead man is able to hear through the static of wit and nostalgia.
He tried but failed to cut a break in the Möbius strip of experience.
He fell on his face trying to lean over the edge.
It was denial made the rain sound like wind.
It was denial caused the poison to be sprayed on the crops.
The dead man has too many examples at hand.
It was a cinch in the time of the piezoelectric crystal-controlled oscillator.
Now the dead man looks in vain for the infinitesimal relay in the printed
    circuit of a microchip made of water.
The dead man knows what is coming.
With pieces of themselves planted, manufactured and cloned, people will
    live what is called "forever."
They will wonder what it was like to have been dead.

2. More About the Dead Man and the Zine

The dead man treasures the treasuries unburied and unlocked in the
    illusions of time.
For now the *Electronic Poetry Review* must shiver at the outskirts of sensibility.
It wobbles and flashes from the outpost of awareness.
It has turned sensibility inside out, there it is.
The dead man is of many minds, always was, and has lived to employ them
    all at once.
That is the dead man nature of the sentence in the indeterminate.
That is the *raison d'être* of the will.
Let the dead man record the demise of free will in the chaos of so many
    choices.
Now we know it all, all the time.
The dead man was happy to be fewer, for all that.
Now he is more than alive as the many.
It was denial that left string theory at loose ends.
It was denial that could not see the unified in disunity, the quantum
    disguised as inertia.
It was eyes, it was the holding action that kept us too close.
Now, as zines populate the cyberworld, the space remains endless.
The dead man pictures the Biggest Bang.
Imagine the imaginary type, the mathematics of a single black hole.
For it was always about the planet, never about us.
The dead man is at peace under the rocketry.
The pure pleasure of pixels lives on, nor all our piety nor wit can cancel the
    binary yes and no of the method.
The dead man is the essence of on and off, of now and later, of forever and
    not at all.
The dead man, at the end, turns a page.

New and Uncollected

The rain
is too heavy a whistle for the certainty of charity.
The moon
throws us off the sense.
The wind
happens at night before you drop off.
The mountains
on them sufferance blisters its skin of paint.
The oceans
in which this happens.
The ash
of which we are made.

The Book of the Dead Man (Dylan's Names)

All I can do is be me, whoever that is.

Bob Dylan

1. About the Dead Man and Dylan's Names

Who were Elston Gunn and Blind Boy Grunt, Bob Landy and Robert
Milkwood Thomas, Tedham Porterhouse and Lucky Wilbury, Boo
Wilbury and Jack Frost, who was Sergei Petrov?
When the Swedish Academy gave him the Nobel, the grumps got huffy and,
wouldn't you know it, the squares got hip.
Ah, but the dead man is the one who knows what it's worth and what it's not
worth, so too the performer who thought up the Never Ending Tour.
The dead man knows that being a grownup means knowing that things end.
The dead man understands in his bones that a lifetime is an interlude, not
yet a flagged sixteenth in a century of whole notes.
To bend the genres as Dylan did meant holding up the sky and spending
his reserves.
We do not ask for propriety when the music starts, nor for civic good, nor
do we await the return of sounds traveling a spherical universe.
We do not ask the music of the spheres to notate the progression of
dissonance to harmony and back, it would take forever.
Who is Bob Dylan, and who was Bob Dylan, and who will have been
Bob Dylan?
It is not incumbent upon the artist to know, nor need a witness come forth.

2. More About the Dead Man and Dylan's Names

The dead man holds that what are known as the blues are only the first
blues, and that hands-up gospel, the lost souls of country, the
rebellious arousal of rock, and the helpless loves of the Great American
Songbook are also the blues.
The dead man will not argue in words, for music always wins.
It's the Dylan of true rhymes, iambics, songs that go on breathing where
others stopped, choruses that became marching orders—not the
staging, but a voice like straw and lungs like an accordion that could
not stop.
The dead man, like Dylan, does not linger in expectation, he too changes
keys and forms, he lightly sings his lines and hums in private, waiting
for the new thing to find him.
No one knows better than the dead man the backward looks of an audience
that craves the all-time favorites.
The dead man is neither a fanboy nor a follower, but is out front with his
ears open.
He knows it when he hears and sees it—music breaking through the noise,
and the analysts in wet shoes.
When lightning hits, the critics simmer and fizzle.
The dead man knows that for the artist who reimagines himself, some luck
is bad luck, as are some places, so why stay there?
Not to remain a Zimmerman, then, who may be the backstage usher who
tells his children he once met you.

The Book of the Dead Man (Corn)

1. About the Dead Man and Corn

When the dead man needs to relax, he listens to the corn.

Listening to the corn grow, the dead man feels alert, then sleepy.

These fields of corn are forever, their tassels flipping in the breeze like a class
    of high school graduates' after commencement.

An ear may whisper to him, the wind sing and the stalks dance.

Happy corn, blanketed by a husk, enveloped by family.

Happy, peaceful corn, aligned and orderly within, yet wild without.

Not a care in the world, joyfully whipped and whipping afield.

Once the dead man detasseled, he peeled, he shucked.

The corn dripped sweetness and the rain washed his sins.

Out of soil and water a seed stood up for itself, while he grew also.

It was a time of family plots, victory gardens, truck farms.

Now he lies and listens to the feed corn of the Midwest, sown from hither to
    yon, stretching time zones as far as an eye can see or an ear hear.

Some corn is food, some will be oil, some antibiotics and some explosive.

This corn rises not for now but for later, not for him but for cattle now and
    him later.

The dead man both mourns and celebrates this indirection, as cattle graze
    the days looking down.

2. More About the Dead Man and Corn

The dead man has come a long way without moving.

Without a knee bend or an arm swing, the dead man has joined the contest between giving and taking.

Long nourished by the harvested, the dead man is replenished now by the plowed-under and the burnt.

He has in his hard memory the feel of the cob.

He can taste a hint of tortilla in the wind, and of bread risen from earth.

How better shall the dead man remember the wind than by the sight of row upon row of corn waving?

How luckier can the kind of man mankind is be, than to have the means to reap vast stores of grain?

The dead man hath been given this day his daily bread.

He feels the beginning and end of time moving across the land from opposite ends.

He feels the earth rumble at the approach of the harvesters.

He is shaken with palsy by the footfalls of the giant pickers.

He burrows, he sinks from sight, he bales the walls of his consciousness around him to stay as he is.

It is fruitless for the dead man to try to fully express his feeling for corn.

When corn speaks, it sighs in the wind and says yesssss.

The Book of the Dead Man (The Bus)

1. About the Dead Man on the Bus

The dead man rides the interstates one-way.

Through the thick bus windows, roadways whip into the past.

Time and again the driver glances up at his mirror to make sure his load is
     behind him.

Taking the off-ramp, the bus rumbles over train tracks and kicks up
     shoulder dust.

It bounces in and out of potholes to the terminal side of town.

The suitcase bins clatter, the door shudders.

A passenger is trying to rewrap a half-eaten sandwich.

Had he a longer stop, he could get a tattoo, pawn his raincoat, learn some
     judo, it's all there.

There's just enough time at the station to sprint to the lunch counter or the
     medicine shelf, take your pick.

Someone may share a sub, but who carries the lotion to ease the pain of a
     sunburnt back?

2. More About the Dead Man on the Bus

Back on the highway, the scenery picks up speed, the road surface drones,
    and the riders drowse.
The driver knows he has an eleven-miles-per-hour tolerance under the
    traffic cameras.
He's "making time," a sort of quantum physics inventor.
He sees the owners of sedans move quickly to the right as he gains on them.
With a broad view at hand, the driver pushes toward a distant turnaround.
Sleeping on a bus is the opposite of sitting still.
Packed with hometown lives, crisscrossing thought and feeling, the
    omniscient and the intimate, the bus is off to everywhere.
The interstate busses offered the military travel on a private's salary.
Or they hitchhiked, though the young dead man hitching was removed by a
    trooper to a bus stop.
Now the dead man rides the bus to have time to write.

The Book of the Dead Man (The Batting Cage)

1. About the Dead Man and the Batting Cage

You know what's coming, and you still can't hit it.

The dead man set the speed at *high,* the pitcher was not permitted beanballs
    or the inside corner of the plate.

It was not as it was for the little lead-off hitter taking one for the team, not
    like that.

The batting cage is a form, a shape, a definition, a physical tautology, an
    insular life of *now,* and again *now,* and *now* yet again.

Snapping overhand, the robotic arm brings it.

You are in the cage to hit line drives, a little arc is best, a liner to the outfield
    will be the top prize.

The mesh ceiling blocks high flies, a grounder is humiliating.

A batter wants to know his next swing will bring rain.

Bring your bat, the cage bats feel waterlogged.

The dead man, a singles hitter, chokes up, he just wants to reach base.

2. More About the Dead Man and the Batting Cage

The dead man, battling a robot hurler, did not wear a helmet.

Even if the arc of its slingshot delivery could go awry, look out.

If only the dead man could predict when a pitch will be a brushback,
    can you?

The runner on first wants to go, does one have to swing?

Imagine, instead, that the strike zone fits you.

You can wait out the wide heat, pay for the plate.

The old batting cages befitted the grit of single-A.

No uniforms, batting gloves, cocky dances or the dreams of parents.

It wasn't when they brought in the fences, juiced the bats and balls, and gave
    up on "get 'em on, get 'em over, get 'em in."

It was when they called the hot dogs "gourmet."

The Book of the Dead Man (Desperate in America)

1. About the Dead Man Desperate in America

The dead man can't stop to sleep.

The daily news lingers late into the nights.

He sees men robbing banks with toy guns.

He sees the impoverished and sickly banging on the prison doors.

The president and his party don't care, they have health insurance that
      includes cuticle control.

They have pensions built from gouging the planet.

They eat oil and coal and stay out of the sun.

They fly the flag of rampant capitalism, the pennants of death to the poor.

2. More About the Dead Man Desperate in America

The perfume they import cannot make them smell better.

They are the privileged in private towers, the idolaters of gold leaf.

They smell of steak sauce and potions taken from people of color who
      hoped to survive.

They make medicine unaffordable.

The dead man hears the creak among the cogs, the slippage of the belt, the
      chugging of the racists and anti-Semites laboring uphill.

Let their time be short, their hollow chests sputter and their teeth fall out,
      for they are the party of death.

A president befitting a mob, a First Family that cares only for itself.

The party in power a-twitter while the opposition has covered the mirrors.

March 25, 2017

The Book of the Dead Man (Dreams and Daydreams)

1. About the Dead Man's Dreams and Daydreams

What's it about, when the dead man sleeps with his eyes open?
The dead man dreams ideas that could change his dreams, but is happy
    to watch.
He sees himself shoulder a baguette like a ladder—it feels dreamy.
He has fallen asleep on a pillow of textile unicorns, they may reappear.
Then he hears the hungry guitar of surrealism and feels the roar of a
    mousetrap—now we're getting somewhere.
Soon fancy will deal him cards depicting, say, cardiac events—that's the ticket.
He knows that a dream is the fantastic that ordains the mundane, the
    infinite that confirms the finite, the whole that informs the discrete.
Even if it be but a fraction of a sensate life, the dreamy existential acted out
    in an oval frame.
His dreams are half the means for feeling what it's all about.
The dead man does not pound his breast or tax the actors to move along.
He keeps his eyes open as worlds transmute, it's the upshot of living on
    two planes.
It suits him that his waking and sleeping are now private studios.
Studio two is for when he has exhausted the words.

2. More About the Dead Man's Dreams and Daydreams

The dead man's way of writing is a new wrinkle on old parchment.
Like you, he was looking for a word in the water, a rune, a code, a clue of
      any kind when he wised up.
He was mopping up after the logicians when he came to his senses.
To the dead man everything glows in the dark.
Hence, daytime is an outpost from where he signals his nighttime mind—
      it's radiocentric.
The dead man's epistemological daggers may skewer egocentric belief.
The ornery temptation still surges within him to move a stone at
      Stonehenge.
The dead man is you, he is not a ghost, nor does he chip away at walls.
Were he a ghost, he could not cover the mortal estate—the grounds of mind
      and no-mind.
It will be known, as baldly as in a broadside, that he has been the recorder of
      a tactile unreality.
His consciousness has been an undercover subversion for those who talk
      back to thought.
His daytimes and nighttimes are preparations.
For him to know means less to him than to know he does not know.

The Book of the Dead Man (Celebrity)

1. About the Dead Man and Celebrity

The dead man registers the minutiae of ego.

He logs the litter and leftovers, the ashes, he counts the folds of a
  handkerchief.

He registers the patina on the statues of generals.

The celebrations of self, once episodic, run on without interstices.

The instep of his shoe sloshes through the blood.

The famous overflow the junk drawer in his head.

Their twit selves have overstocked the Internet scrapyard.

The faux reality, the life-force deformed, the death rattle rage to be
  remarkable.

He crinkles the tabloids to make an alternate story, he celebrates the cutups
  of Dada.

He blinks at the foil of talk show guests selling penny candy.

2. More About the Dead Man and Celebrity

The pixels became pokes, the pokes became detachable grams, the Big Bang
  became a screenshot.

The dead man thinks it was more when it was less.

He regrets that he straightened the typewriter letters.

He does not regret covering his tracks with misdirection.

If it was called for, he aligned, he amalgamated, he harmonized at a distance,
  but he was not one of them.

He, like you, learned to pass, and did pass and kept going.

He shot the stars from the firmament to become the Walk of Fame.

His interest in the hams and grandstanders was that of a leaf in the wind.

When it fell, it was trampled by the rush to residuals.

The dead man sold the same poem twice to one magazine, it was that good.

The Book of the Dead Man (The Election)

1. About the Dead Man and the Election

The dead man ate and went to bed.

The morning after the election, he was once again uneasy.

He worried about who now had the ear of the president-elect.

He had qualms about the cocksure ex-professor back in vogue.

He swam in a flood of late reports from the cults, cliques and cabals.

He felt the bewilderment of those who thought much of the country an undifferentiated flyover.

He thought back to the calamities of "the best and the brightest."

He had watched the humanities wither on the ivy.

He saw again an aggregate of interests shattered by single-issue voters.

2. More About the Dead Man and the Election

He, too, heard the plans of the high-flyers, the salt of the earthbound, the prideful *summa cum laud-ies* and dishonest Abes, the impetuous fresh-faced and the grumps against change.

He has felt the heat of the self-righteous and the bully-pulpit bullies.

He has seen the best of Congress sapped in the hunt for cash.

The dead man is not surprised, he is never surprised, those who know they live in the pre-posthumous will never be surprised.

He does not forget that minorities everywhere have had to know what's up and where to stand.

The question recurs, whether to stay or go.

There will be no absolution for the ideologues, the for-hire celebrities, the vain talking heads, the provincial dailies of the cities, the rich who stiff workers.

The dead man does not want to say that he is better than anyone, and Mercutio had it right, but *this?*

A nation ruled by the wickedly rich.

The Book of the Dead Man (His Papers)

1. About the Dead Man's Papers

The dead man remembers paper.
He remembers roller-skate keys and fruit-box scooters, typewriter ribbons
    and swamp coolers, and lots and lots of paper.
Paper stained by words and telltale commas.
He could spot talent in a writer's commas.
There were meanings, there were diagrams on the ball field that told the
    players where to run, there were lines in the dirt that paralyzed
    a chicken.
There was crumpled paper holding words that would never be released.
And there were blackouts in the national files so that documents attesting to
    the criminality of officials became graphic illustrations of barrier art.
The dead man tore paper in the fashion of atomic dispersals.
He burned paper in the fashion of cremation.
He balled up the good ideas that were too late and the personal confessions
    of friends.

2. More About the Dead Man's Papers

He took the papers of the famous, and what he knew, to his grave.
The dead man blots paper of its blood and its tears.
He tapes together the halves that were torn apart in anger and secretes them.
He relieves the insecure.
He drops a dime on the drafts of the dull, the lightweights, the minor
    laureates.
The dead man loves the shredder and incinerator.
He buries treasure but leaves no maps.
Everything in dead man's space is an *X*, you yourself can name it.
There is a word for each *X*, a site specific, an open vise.
Stick your neck out if you like.

The Book of the Dead Man (If & When)

1. About the Dead Man If & When

If and when the dead man gets his pup tent up, he will love the heavy
     splatter-sound of rain on the canvas.
If and when the dead man recalls the past, he will linger there.
If he crawls out after the storm, he will have to grow up.
A dead-man-in-waiting becoming a grownup dead man means meat and
     blankets, drums and mops, paint and glue.
If he wants to come out from under, he will end up knowing the character of
     things and of actions, but not of art.
If he looks for the soul, he will find only electrochemistry.
For the dead man has been a magician of milk and grease, and he knows the
     makeup of thin air.
Hence, he blots ink with his sleeve to make from an abstraction an event.
It is the balance between dark matter and sticky stuff that keeps the
     astronomers at bay.
It is the space between creation and doom that festers with the life force.

2. More About the Dead Man If & When

If and when he examines his father's papers, he will reach vainly for an
    immigrant's life of bullets and orchards.
If one's son was to become an American, it meant no looks back, no
    crawling in the ditches, for it was more than it seemed.
Likewise, if the dead man's verbal shenanigans seem to you less than
    pensive, you have taken the shortcut.
If his random wherewithal seems to you indefinite, you have overlooked the
    joy at the core of his not knowing.
If and when he changes his mind about entropy, he will let you know.
In the meantime, he has aged—it is so.
He does not fault the precious and specious, nor mock the woebegone and
    goody-two-shoes.
Heraclitus and he have had a talk about the absence of the present, that
    collective hypnosis of "what was it?"
The dead man is the seer of what it was that still is.
He is a lever, he considers the past a work in progress.

The Book of the Dead Man (The Fountain Pen)

1. About the Dead Man's Bar Mitzvah

The dead man, turning thirteen, received several gift-boxed fountain pens.
Also, a heavyweight suitcase to pack for college.
Also, wallets smelling of unopened repositories where there could someday
    be cash.
In fact, he wore the look of the oblivious, he relished his tunnel vision, he
    was doomed to hit the wall like a muggy bat.
"Today, I am a man," was a demolition to be absorbed while looking back.
The evenings of late walks to nowhere became late drives to water's edge.
His innermost solitude soaked up the flood of his experiences.
He thought little of who he was, while the ink dried in the fountain pens.
It would not have been seemly to say, "Today, I am a dead-man-in-waiting."
The road from town shimmered on the outskirts—no clue.

2. More About the Dead Man's Bar Mitzvah

If later he knew himself, he was not saying.
He still had the pens that drew spirals reaching for legibility, the rubberized
    ones for their grip and quiet, the one with the nozzle of four colors.
He thought of the residue in one-room-schoolhouse inkwells, and studied
    the map of doomed villages.
His true idiom lay unseen as he chewed his pen, of a mind with his best
    teachers.
Steam in a kitchen, splinters in the lumber, the itch of a sling and the
    instability of crutches—such small life lessons.
He, like you, was raised not to know . . . but came to know.
He is wont to exercise the scrutiny of a seashell for which the life of the deep
    comes and goes.
He is keen to wax ecstatic in the mild tones of a baritone horn.
He is, like you, the cryptologist of his youth.
Like you, he was a child when he became a man.

The Book of the Dead Man (Joyous Dead Man)

1. Joyous Dead Man (The Ultimate Subtext)

The dead man renews the end of the world.

For him. For you.

He sees the queue inching forward, resolute if banal, eternal if in parts.

He is there to view the squiggle as it is, the snaky perambulations of those
     desperate to depart.

Those wishing to live forever in the abstraction of time.

Nor to meet oneself returning from the future, nor to draw forth the past.

Nor to become such energy as may coalesce in an eye or tongue, nor as spit
     or phlegm, nor as paper or ink.

Never to become a wing or a pebble, nor any voiceless matter.

Never to be the diaspora of minute particles.

The dead man is not like that.

His living has been of the moment, his days and nights have been long, his
     life has been quick to the horizon.

Pass by the dead man, for he knoweth both sides.

Make room, for he will be molting, flaking and peeling in the providence of
     the encrusted.

2. More Joyous Dead Man (The Ultimate Subtext)

The dead man has witnessed the early finality of beheadings and suicides.

He has welcomed home the soldiers who now envy the headless.

He has looked in many places, met the quizzical stare of passport control,
    affirmed his itchy feet to the agent.

Shall he now be exiled among the anonymous in long coats?

Can he swim in the wake of the big boats?

Will he always duck in time?

And does he only imagine that the queue is speeding up?

The dead man would hang from the hands of Big Ben if his weight could
    undo the news.

He lives, like you, in a nation of consternation.

He was well worried, he was worried sick, he took to bed and catatonia.

When he came to, he was the new dead man.

Impervious because his escape hatch is the future.

He handled the morning and went out in the sun to stand in line.

The Book of the Dead Man (His Whistling)

1. About the Dead Man and His Whistling

May it be apt for the dead man to explain himself.

There was carefree whistling, whistling to hoot at the inept toreador,
    whistling in appreciation, whistling past the graveyard.

The dead man's whistling was born in youth of oblivious joy, the pathway
    ahead, and somewhere to get to or not, all in good time.

It was not the summons of a tight-lip tweet, nor a two-fingers-in-the-mouth
    heads-up, nor the trilling of a bird.

He was not calling, nor keeping the day at bay, nor was he more ambitious
    than the insensible sole of his shoe.

His whistling was music for the cloud parade and the light pressure of rain,
    for he walked out whatever the time or weather.

Like the undertaker who whistles while he works, he was doubly engaged.

The funeral home was next to the grade school.

The camera store kept its window lit all night.

They were playing cards at the firehouse, the hoses curled in sleep.

2. More About the Dead Man and His Whistling

How different were he one of them, who rode the bumpers to fires, who
    closed late the hardware store, who polished the coffins.
The young man did not have to be more.
A life of if and when.
The whistle in a squeal of delight, the screech of wet brakes and edgy
    downshifting, the kettle's high register—to come awake in the youthful
    miasma.
Past midnight, turning the beat-frequency oscillator dial to find a signal
    between the static and whistles.
The slide whistle of comedy, the wooden ball bobbing in the plastic toy
    whistle, the highs of singer Yma Sumac and trumpeter Maynard
    Ferguson, the crystal-breaking scores of the Kenton band, were
    reaching beyond the death rattle.
If it strained ears—well, lifting the future from the past, the hinge squeaks.
It may seem absurd to others that the dead man is alive.
Somewhere in the past, the footsteps of The Whistler, that omniscient radio
    host of crime and fate.
No words to lessen the feeling.

The Book of the Dead Man (Milk)

One must imagine Sisyphus happy.

Albert Camus

1. About the Dead Man and Milk

The dead man's imagination contains the future.

The logicians will be shutting their eyes when they lose in the past the
　　proofs of his mind's eye.

The quantum physicists will be donning mittens when they see how their
　　presence distorted the present.

Friends of the ethicists will be hiding their pals' knives when the purveyors
　　of ends and means overcome them.

When, that is, ethics is shown to be a luxury of circumstance.

The issue before us is, therefore, did Sisyphus drink milk as a child?

Does that explain his innocent persistence?

Does it account for his happiness absent success?

Was it a protective coating for the inner life to come?

One does not bypass the emotional resonance of one's primary elixir.

2. More About the Dead Man and Milk

The dead man, like Sisyphus, can be followed.
He knows, whatever the salvationist says, that entropy trumps time.
He is at peace with depletions and erasures, and he smiles to recall the
        sensuous milk bottles once left at the door.
He has run behind the ice truck in the heat.
Stay with me, he says, follow me to the new worlds of the mind.
The dead man did not need a scrapbook, nor keep a journal, nor lean into
        the future with his hair combed.
If it rusted, if it melted, if it evaporated, that was not the end of it.
The dead man acts anonymously in several places at once.
He shreds the records and prescriptions, and dissolves the pills.
He has gone on drinking milk to get over things.

The Book of the Dead Man (Silence)

1. About the Dead Man and Silence

The dead man has cultivated an alien silence.

Amid cacophony, his deepest ear remains at low tide, his insides go quiet.

He has turned down the amp, curbed the snaky squeal of the mic, and asks
     now a favor of the audience.

He asks the audience not to applaud early.

For he holds within him a solitude within crowds, a sanguinity in air and a
     buoyancy at sea.

To have been this way when younger would have meant no schooling, no
     job, no offers for his soul.

In geezerhood and beyond, the dead man has thrown a blanket over the
     make-work dissonance of the national treadmill.

Humor in the face of the inevitable has been fundamental to an Existential
     Absurdist like the dead man.

That, and earplugs.

2. More About the Dead Man and Silence

To the dead man, silence is the norm, interrupted at intervals.

The dead man listens for silence while the earth rumbles.

He hears the molten lava churning in the planetary core.

He registers the interruptions of wind assailing the trees.

He does not seek it in the traffic of the ether or in sleep where the
     machinery of ears makes dreams of bees and swordplay.

To know pure silence, he will have to stop his pulse, neutralize the magnetic
     pull of each particle in the universe, and just stop.

To just stop will mean no more swish or fizzle or bubbling, no delusion of
     an interval.

Then, the music.

In the meantime, don't ask, he won't hear you.

The Book of the Dead Man (Work)

1. About the Dead Man and Work

The dead man renews his license, his permit and his papers, for the dead
    man likes to be paid.
The dead man's brain must warm up to work, as a bulb burns inside itself to
    produce light.
The deep-sea fisherman, at risk among the icy nets, looks ahead.
The shaft miner, descending, day by day maps the underground.
Work is not talk, and the dead man has heard the veteran, recalling a
    mission, swallow his words.
He sees the farmer plodding in the static of muddy afternoons.
He sees the clerk restocking the dank basement of the dry goods store.
He hears the shot of the roofer's nail gun, the whine of the builder's bandsaw.
He sees the tradesman favor work shirts in the quietude of retirement.
The dead man prefers the labor movement to the literary movement.

2. More About the Dead Man and Work

The store owner expected to add his son to the sign, it seemed safe.
The carpenter, plumber and electrician got theirs into the unions, it
    seemed secure.
They did not think sweat a perfume or labor a romance.
Their work, to them, was workaday.
The dead man respects both the sore shoulder and the headache, the
    foreman and the apprentice.
Likewise, he honors jointly the chef and the fry cook, the bird colonel and
    the dogface.
The dead man knows that workers' compensation applies equally to the
    mental hospital and the surgical ward.
The dead man has heard the oil worker spit and the steelworker cough.
He hears, too, the oboist weep in a high register of having to quit before the
    instrument kills him.
It takes the dead man to see how hard it can be to sing or dance.

The Book of the Dead Man (Van Gogh)

My step is unsteady.

Vincent to Theo

1. About the Dead Man and Van Gogh

The dead man lives with the shell of Van Gogh's ear and a nautilus brought
    in by the tide.
He wrinkles the skin of his hand until he can see in it the black indecency of
    crows in Vincent's wheat field.
He sees the self-portrait stare that shook the artist's will to live.
If the canvas were not a window, if the paints were not blood, if the frame
    were not a prison, then one could put it aside.
The dead man's easel triangulates eye and heart to a pinpoint on the horizon.
Van Gogh's workman's boots, his oversize sunflowers—these swallow the
    dead man looking.
His mulberry tree pounds its chest, just try to walk past.
His pink roses shout, his wheat stacks give birth, his thatched cottages
    tremble, his crabs dance.
His bedroom in Arles remains askew, his still lives are everything but.
Every stroke a thrust.

2. More About the Dead Man and Van Gogh

Vincent's crows are not crows but crows stuck to thick air.
A chair Vincent paints is not a chair, but a Van Gogh chair.
There is a sky, there is earth, there is toil in the wrinkled sunlight.
Somewhere a sea, and sometimes light.
The thick strokes and layered memory of his correspondence were
        themselves the hoarse equivalent of the painterly.
It is all Vincent, a clawing topography of an inner life.
A calligraphy that oozed.
The dead man, too, has turned his life into his livelihood at a price.
It is more to have swallowed absinthe and digitalis, to be hypergraphical and
        sun-beaten, and to know the margins of bipolarity.
It is more to have suffered in yellow.

The Book of the Dead Man (Water)

1. About the Dead Man and Water

Where the Atlantic cuffs rocks at land's end, there a man may be reminded
    that things are not what they seem.
The splashing at makeshift barriers anywhere also brings to mind the low
    tide peeling itself as it leaves.
In the dead man's brain are as many canals as has the planet.
In the hollow of the dead man's chest, like a boat in blood, his heart bumps,
    again and always again, the future.
He bumped the tide to go out, now he bumps it to reach land.
A geezer-in-waiting from the day he was born, now the flesh of his arms
    hangs like packets of dry oak leaves in winter.
The dead man is not what he appears to those who think they can see time.
He has his chin up, he is chipper, he towels his wit to bag a listener.
Nor shall the dead man reveal himself to the historical registers.
He sees no reason to bag the past.

2. More About the Dead Man and Water

To the dead man, all biographers wear gloves, touch not.
And the autobiographical noise mounts from people trying to remember
    themselves.
Metaphor, a way to think few now recall, long junked.
One sees a few bubbles rising from the dumps after a rainfall.
It is the life of the mind gasping from the disintegrating pages of
    discarded books.
The family tree, shrunken, is a vine.
Oh leaves that became folios, oh the marine existence of wood and cloth in
    the acidic baths of papermaking.
It is still true that we never step into the same soak twice.
Inside the dead man are the ducts and streams of a life-force field.
An invisible barrier, a privacy at sea.

The Book of the Dead Man (Poetry Readings)

1. About the Dead Man and Poetry Readings

Live from your bookstore, it's the dead man, imagine!

He winces at the nervous reader who sipped water, then slammed the glass
     on the table.

The one who threw up into the I-Thou pastries, it's a famous story.

He has listened to those who had answers and those who did not, those who
     were who they were and those who were, for an evening, someone else.

In the fictive world, we could sit at peace.

We were smarter, centered, we lived awhile in our own worlds.

Yes, the dead man has been known to giggle when answering questions.

The dead man is serious about the Absurd.

2. More About the Dead Man and Poetry Readings

It happens that we can be more alive, an hour at a time.

Oh, he saw some of you scanning the titles of shelved books behind
     the lectern.

He saw you peek at your watch.

But he also saw you slow to leave when you could not uncouple yourself
     from the emotions of no-time.

The world of the word.

The world of cerebral audacity, of language birthing, of vocal nuance, of
     angst, comedy, chutzpah, the swanky and the gritty.

Also, the inexpressible beauty of the tautological.

He admits he is not a fan of those who bleed all over themselves for applause.

The Book of the Dead Man (The Metaphysician)

1. About the Dead Man Metaphysician

One must live a long time to inhabit the moment, which has about it the
    residue of those who were lost.
The dead man's speculative philosophy smacks of defiance.
It was never a retirement.
His metaphysics have been stand-alone, not those of the prophet, the
    clairvoyant, the born-again, the daydreamer or the pundit.
Neither are they a one-off.
The dead man's is a timeless existence, he is not alarmed by the entropic.
Like you, he is a metaphysician, exploring what it means to be.
Is it a solace to know that your energy will propagate?
The dead man has declared, "I am; therefore, I think."
In the studies of the dead man there can be no conclusions.

2. More About the Dead Man Metaphysician

The dead man will not say, with Socrates, that the unexamined life is not
    worth living.
One may be a master of things without listing them.
The dead man likes pedestrian shoes, utilitarian lamps and inexpensive
    clockworks.
You see what it means.
The dead man's sensory life undercuts the reductive and hyperbolic
    biographies of the famous, those tomes of the temporary.
He does not memorialize the present.
He takes his medicine, he registers the lab reports.
His stiffening heart valve murmurs its song.
He limps a little, favors this knee or that, unlocks his fingers.
However late it may appear, his obit will be premature.

The Book of the Dead Man (Writer's Block)

1. About the Dead Man and Writer's Block

The dead man sees his writing going nowhere.

Seeing his writing going nowhere, the dead man follows it.

To cafés and bars, to the corner market, to bus stops where it sits limp-
    kneed, swaying, awaiting him with a twisted smile.

The dead man's writing has shone in dim light.

The dead man's heart has broken from the finality of the period.

Forever to wonder if it should be a comma—or a dash.

The dead man's heart is a muscle hidden deep in his mind.

When leaves are trembling, the floor beams quiet, the dead man stays up
    late and wonders that the world sleeps beyond the edge of his chair,
    beyond the lip of the sill.

The dead man cannot find a word to describe the rattle of bones in distant
    subways, or the shaking of branches that nobody will hear.

In such cases, the dead man sometimes settles for "O."

The dead man wonders about editors.

The dead man still reads the daily paper.

The dead man does not keep notes.

The dead man does not know the scene from the seen, the line from the
    page, or the beginning from the end.

The dead man's critiques smell of must and dead flowers.

The dead man does not keep notes, his notes keep him.

2. More About the Dead Man and Writer's Block

Two buckets of water and a moldy mop—thirteen chickens in a large
    black cage.
The dead man knows such things intimately, and sometimes the knowing
    is enough.
The dead man knows his p's from his q's.
With ink on his fingers, the dead man writes his name on his forehead.
The dead man sees the sun rise and, believing in the infinite possibility,
    calls it a fish.
The dead man hears rumors, and so becomes a rumor himself, a whisper of
    water from ear to ear, a gospel of gossip, the anecdote of an artichoke.
The dead man knows there is always a war.
His eyes hold sleep at arm's length.
If ever uncertain, the dead man can crawl behind a comma or become his
    own parenthesis.
Only the dead man truly knows the referent of "it."
The dead man does not differentiate creative writing from a hole in his head.

The Book of the Dead Man (The Angel of Apocalypse)

1. About the Dead Man and the Angel of Apocalypse

The dead man thrashes to escape the terror that traps him in his bedcovers.
If its wings blanket the sky, it must be called monstrous.
It is an Age when the angelic, misshapen and grotesque, is no longer credible.
Still the apocalyptic angel arrives in the zone of the zombie and android, in a
    province without the providential.
And the ogre whose bad breath wilts the sheets.
And the massive bats who claw the blankets into knots.
The dead man struggles to free his legs and staggers to the window to see
    beyond the shade.
If he fights or runs, he remains the prey of the unheavenly.
There will be warfare on steroids and bulbous Satans in suits.
Thus arrives the pituitary event whereby armies block the sun.

2. More About the Dead Man and the Angel of Apocalypse

The likes of Godzilla and Frankenstein's giant are but storytime playthings.
Ghouls, phantoms and spirits, the Minotaur, Charybdis—toys for a plywood
    tabletop.
Bring on Medusa, the Hydra, the reptilian, the alien, the Greek and Assyrian
    sphinxes—for they, too, shall be departed.
For they disappear when the dead man shuts his eyes.
Yet there comes, still, the specter of an all-encompassing human frailty, and
    the catastrophic angel who sucks up the light.
The dead man tugs at his blankets as if to reach the surface.
The horror is everywhere, it issues an inanimate howl as he attempts to cover
    his closed eyes.
By day, the dead man shines a light on the monstrous gods and their minions.
He is unblinking before them, untouchable until nightfall.
Then come the inescapable flights from the apocalyptic, and the run from the
    Rilkean bad boys born of a slumbering chemistry.

The Book of the Dead Man (That Wednesday)

1. About the Dead Man and That Wednesday

It was the middle of the workweek when the dead man checked out.

It happened at the hub of activity, the midsection of a salary.

Midweek was yellowing in the high-floor windows.

He was, on Wednesday, the pivot of a utilitarian seesaw.

Perched between up and down, a diameter in some half arc of industry, he was.

He was not sure what came next and what to trash.

So he up and walked away.

No one had quit on a Wednesday—papers stacked in the in-box.

He gave notice by waving as he left.

Like Bartleby, he waxed minimally on desire and wanted out.

The pens bled, the stationary wilted, the desk chair rolled to the side.

They thought he would return on Thursday.

2. More About the Dead Man and That Wednesday

The door hinge squeaked twice as he exited.

They recall now the dead man's quietude, his odd composure, his bearing
    bled of angst.

They think now they should have foreseen his making tracks.

It seems he drank water at the cooler instead of talking.

He had often swiveled in his chair, it was a sign, as was his back to the room.

His reasons will be sought in vain on company websites and in office
    photographs.

He was just tired of facing the outside.

Weary of expectancy, of strategies and alchemical jargon.

Everyone in ant lines under the corporate boot.

Yet his childhood lived on, impervious to analysis.

They were lost to him who had been real on Monday and Tuesday.

He spoke of this into his sleeve, then threw his voice under the desk and
    walked out.

The Book of the Dead Man (The Uprising)

1. About the Dead Man and the Uprising

From camps deep in the woods, a signal—scratchy, intermittent.

From a notch in a cave wall that tricks from wind a scrawny whistle.

From a specimen of the past expunging a trapped stink.

The smallest stirring has weight to those who live beneath or apart, hidden
       or overlooked, flattened by events, semiconscious after work.

Now the electorate, heretofore muted, puny and frail, cocks its ears.

You want details, here are details.

The dead man was among the young people who took to the street.

Dead men and dead women went alongside in multitudinous numbers.

They wore tee shirts and djellabas, turbans and baseball caps, letter jackets
       and yarmulkes.

They colored the walls of gray buildings as they marched.

2. More About the Dead Man and the Uprising

There was a moment before the pot boiled, a little simmering was all.

The surface was barely stirred, the tide rolled in and out.

The dead man saw the officials waiting it out in good eateries.

Pardon me, said the dead man, not without irony.

Pardon my hand, up from the grave, pardon my detached legs on the move.

The dead man lay among those who had been dispatched.

Something moved, the earth's crust cracked, it was a crowd route-stepping
      in the street.

The dead man thinks you'll get yours, guilty and innocent alike.

The dead man, like you, is at fault.

While it happens, his blameless half sings and dances—of mournful
      pleasures and mindless joy.

For the songs of fate are playful, mischievous, genial and victorious.

The Book of the Dead Man (Mayhem)

1. About the Dead Man and Mayhem

Did the dead man say "mayhem" when he meant "mayflies," "war time"
when he meant "more time?"
Did he get it wrong, or was he trying to be upbeat?
Did he say nine when he meant none, did he say it's all white when he
meant to ask what?
The dead man ages, words yellow like candlelight, and meanings shift.
A tree he thought evergreen is undressed by a wind gust, how could that
happen?
Something is going on underneath the orator who raises a lukewarm finger
to shush the planet.
The constant rasp of parliamentary idiocy is like low-flying geese, circling.
Meanwhile, petals, twigs and feathers are being dislodged early.
Meanwhile, foliage and forests go into the past, and migrating birds go awry.
Did the dead man say "scream" when he meant "cream," is that how things
changed?
He meant deep when he said sleep, he meant what it was when he said
what it is.
The dead man will leave a small footprint, a few photos of his several looks,
some writing without the key, worn shoes, unclean laundry.
His tenderness will go without words, his favorite colors will be squeezed
between louder shades, he will feel more and say less.

2. More About the Dead Man and Mayhem

Before the kiss of the earth and the blanket of the sky, there were tactile
  histories.
The dead man lived low on islands, protuberant on peninsulas, uphill in the
  foothills, on prairie, in desert, in heat and cold, in wet and dry.
As time passed, the light winked.
There were hints in a rain burst, nuances in a freeze.
He paused on the sidewalk, sniffing the industrial air, it was age.
His handwriting grew so simple it was thought illegible, then obscure.
History looked like a spiral, destined to be repeated on other planes.
And friends from childhood had traveled through time, that's it.
A trace of frankincense, a face, a siren, a scrape or scraping—memory spun
  him behind and ahead.
Where the land had kissed the water, the water had kissed back, that was
  how the planet shook its body.
That was it, he would not perish but be a man of parts, a cool dude, at last a
  cool dude.
Sitting at a café, looking at the Rock of Gibraltar, that's how things are.
He says he has to go have his picture taken, when he is just going to the
  men's room.

The Book of the Dead Man (Dead Man's Float)

1. About the Dead Man's Float

The closest thing to the dead man poems is synchronicity.

The closest thing to the dead man poems is chaos.

The closest thing, the closest thing, is your heart in pieces.

You hobbyists, this is not your hobby.

The closest thing to the dead man poems is a missing airplane.

The closest things to the dead man poems are lost memories.

The dead man poems are for those who know they are living in the
     pre-posthumous.

Who can see that, once cows and bulls in the china shop, they have become
     invisible.

Whose old haunts are weeds.

Can you be happy like pliers, the smile of the open jaws, yes someday you
     will be.

Can you be putty in the hands of the vise, of course you can.

These poems are to put you at peace, if you are on the way.

Sisyphus the usable fiction, Apollo of the fictive sun, Medusa of the
     appearances, your time is up.

2. More About the Dead Man's Float

The closest thing to a dead man poem is a cul-de-sac.

The closest thing to a dead man poem is a nude descending a staircase.

The closest thing to a dead man poem is one hand clapping.

You professionals, this is not your profession.

The closest things to the dead man poems are ashes and tea leaves.

The closest things to the dead man poems are Machu Picchu and Volubilis.

The dead man poems are for those who know they are the artifacts of
force fields.

Who can neither forget nor revisit.

They are the things they have touched that now speak to them, who
else knows?

Can you be content to float on radio waves, to flutter in the leaves, to
burrow with the mole, you know how.

Can you detect what gums up the works of the heart, it's a skill.

These poems are to lighten your shadow and polish your intuition.

Zeus of the thunderbolt, Mars of the battlefield ambulance, Neptune of the
scuttled, your fictive hubris is conclusively kaput.

Index of First Lines

In an evening of icicles, tree branches crackling as they break frozen sap, a gull's
bark shattering on snow, the furnace turned down for the night, the corpse
air without exits—here the dead man reenters his fever, 83

In the curvature of space, in the ox yoke of industry, half-encircled by the arm
of the rainbow or earthly in the curled palm of an open hand, the dead man
lives ahead and behind, 173

It was the middle of the workweek when the dead man checked out, 306

Like the hero of *The Trial*, the dead man is and is not, 125

Live from your bookstore, it's the dead man, imagine!, 301

Low sounds roll over the dead man in his cardboard box, 116

May it be apt for the dead man to explain himself, 291

Mornings, he keeps out the world awhile, the dead man, 266

Music stirs the dead man to nostalgia, he bubbles, he ferments, 63

Now the dead man quivers with increasing abnormality, 130

One must live a long time to inhabit the moment, which has about it the
residue of those who were lost, 302

Out of a suitcase of discards there came dead lilacs and a dead Abe Lincoln,
and the dead man was there to see it, 113

Patrick "Eel" O'Brian, the dead man has been following you, 255

Perhaps it is not so important that the dead man lives, 73

Picture the dead man in two rooms in the northwest corner of his being, 224

Reactive, resurgent, the dead man welcomes a steamy updraft, 94

Seven young men went looking to beat up a Hispanic and found one and killed
him, and the dead man will speak of it, 234

Strange to say it, but the dead man needs sleep, 51

Ten to one, the one in question made it home safely, 150

When the dead man feels pangs, he thinks he is in the Sudan or Somalia when the crops failed, 120

When the dead man feels the heat, he thinks he's in the spotlight, 71

When the dead man hears the thunderous steps of an ant, he feels eager, 49

When the dead man hears thunder, he thinks someone is speaking, 33

When the dead man itches, he thinks he has picked up a splinter, 98

When the dead man joins up, he monitors the monitors, 190

When the dead man needs to relax, he listens to the corn, 275

When the dead man opens himself up, he is blown about, showered, shed, scattered, dismantled, diluted and diffused, not discarded, 134

When the dead man rises from bed, time smiles, 161

When the dead man sees a rock, he remembers the hidden ball trick, 21

When the dead man splays his arms and legs, he is a kind of Medusa, 29

When the dead man stands on one leg, he thinks he's a heron, 102

When the dead man thinks himself exposed, he puts on a mask, 53

When the dead man throws up, he thinks he sees his inner life, 13

When the dead man wants to deaden his brain, he surfs the channels, 186

When the dead man wears his camouflage suit, he hides in plain sight, 188

When the dead man writes a poem, he immediately writes another one, 164

When the dead man's ankle breaks, he is stoical, 17

When the dead man's arm goes numb, he thinks an emotion is leaving, 91

When the dead man's skin turns black and blue, he thinks it is winter, 45

Where the Atlantic cuffs rocks at land's end, there a man may be reminded that things are not what they seem, 300

Who were Elston Gunn and Blind Boy Grunt, Bob Landy and Robert Milkwood Thomas, Tedham Porterhouse and Lucky Wilbury, Boo Wilbury and Jack Frost, who was Sergei Petrov? 273

Will the dead man speak? Speak, says the lion, and the dead man makes the
    sound of a paw in the dirt, 19

Within range of the sodden fanfare, 112

Would it have been news if space aliens had landed? 177

You know what's coming, and you still can't hit it, 279

About the Author

Marvin Bell was born in New York City, August 3, 1937. Often redefining his poetics from book to book, he is the creator of the Dead Man and Dead Man Resurrected poems, and has been called "ambitious without pretension." Reviewers have said, "Marvin Bell enlarges our understanding of what poetry can do," and "Bell's poems, beyond their formal mastery, constitute an admirable project whose interrogations run deep." He is known also for his many collaborations with other artists and for his down-to-earth teaching. He and his wife, Dorothy, live in Iowa City, Iowa, and for the last thirty-four years also partly in Port Townsend, Washington. Their sons, Nathan and Jason, live in Signal Mountain, Tennessee, and New York City, respectively.

Poetry is vital to language and living. Since 1972, Copper Canyon Press has published extraordinary poetry from around the world to engage the imaginations and intellects of readers, writers, booksellers, librarians, teachers, students, and donors.

WE ARE GRATEFUL FOR THE MAJOR SUPPORT PROVIDED BY:

THE PAUL G. ALLEN
FAMILY FOUNDATION

TO LEARN MORE ABOUT UNDERWRITING
COPPER CANYON PRESS TITLES,
PLEASE CALL 360-385-4925 EXT. 103

WE ARE GRATEFUL FOR THE MAJOR SUPPORT PROVIDED BY:

Anonymous

Jill Baker and Jeffrey Bishop

Anne and Geoffrey Barker

Donna and Matt Bellew

John Branch

Diana Broze

The Beatrice R. and Joseph A.
    Coleman Foundation Inc.

The Currie Family Fund

Laurie and Oskar Eustis

Mimi Gardner Gates

Nancy Gifford

Gull Industries Inc. on behalf of
    William True

The Trust of Warren A. Gummow

Carolyn and Robert Hedin

Bruce Kahn

Phil Kovacevich and Eric Wechsler

Lakeside Industries Inc. on behalf
    of Jeanne Marie Lee

Maureen Lee and Mark Busto

Peter Lewis

Ellie Mathews and Carl Youngmann
    as The North Press

Hank Meijer

Gregg Orr

Petunia Charitable Fund and
    adviser Elizabeth Hebert

Gay Phinny

Suzie Rapp and Mark Hamilton

Emily and Dan Raymond

Jill and Bill Ruckelshaus

Cynthia Sears

Kim and Jeff Seely

Richard Swank

Dan Waggoner

Barbara and Charles Wright

Caleb Young as C. Young Creative

The dedicated interns and
    faithful volunteers of
    Copper Canyon Press

The Chinese character for poetry is made up of two parts:
"word" and "temple." It also serves as pressmark for
Copper Canyon Press.

The poems are set in Minion Pro.
Book design and composition by Phil Kovacevich.